HIDDEN FACES OF THE MAYA

ALTI
PUBLISHING

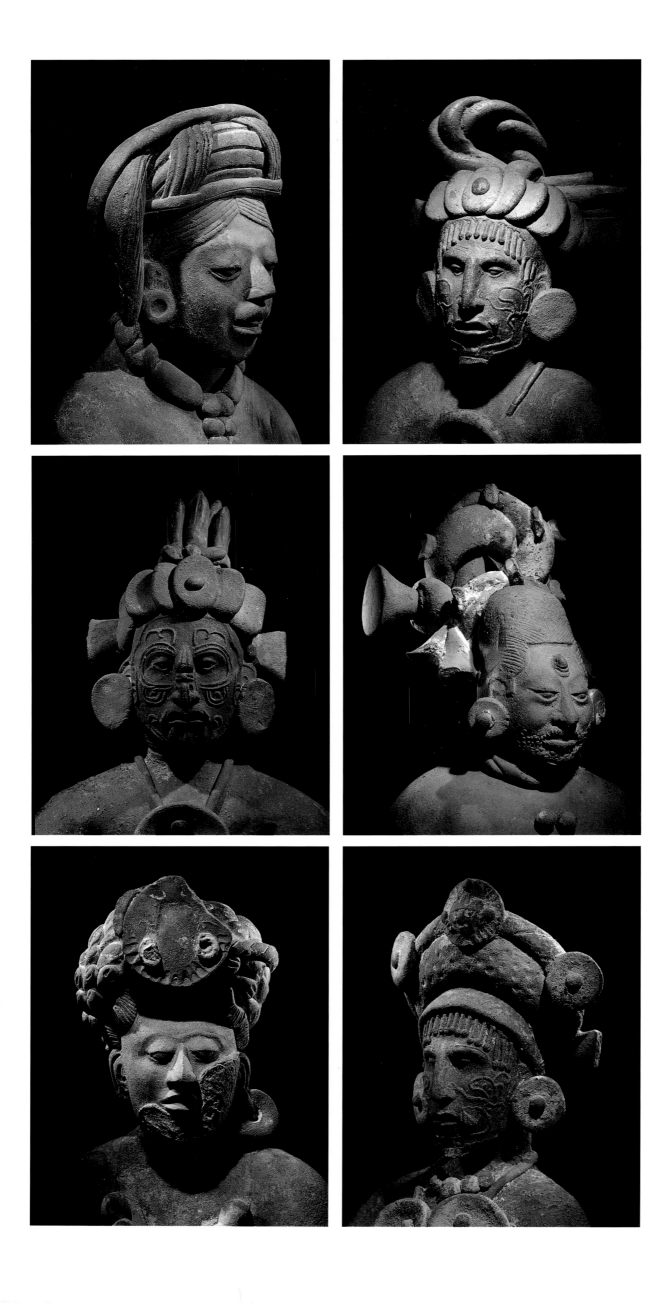

HIDDEN FACES OF THE
MAYA

Linda Schele

Photography
Jorge Pérez de Lara

Presentation
Román Piña Chan

Texts
Linda Schele

Photography
Jorge Pérez de Lara

Presentation
Román Piña Chan

Graphic design
Martín J. García-Urtiaga T.
Lucila Flores de Clavé

Editorial coordination
Jorge Pérez de Lara

Translation of texts
Jorge Pérez de Lara

Editorial production
Maite García-Urtiaga T.
Martín J. García-Urtiaga T.
Impetus Comunicación S.A. de C.V.

Photography assistants
César Peralta
Mariana Kahlo
Victor Pérez de Lara

First edition, 1997
© Impetus Comunicación S.A de C.V.
© Texts, Linda Schele

ISBN 1-883051-16-9

COVER PHOTOGRAPH: see page 171; BACK COVER PHOTOGRAPH: see page 122;
PHOTOGRAPHS ON PAGE 2: a) see page 34; b) see page 78, c) see page 76;
d) see page 44; e) see page 74; f) see page 69;
PHOTOGRAPH ON PAGE 6: see page 73;
PHOTOGRAPH ON PAGE 8: see page 25;
PHOTOGRAPH ON PAGE 12: *Yale University Art Galery,
Stephen Carlton Clark, B. A. 1903 Fund.*

Printed in Singapore byToppan Printing Co.

ACKNOWLEDGMENTS

The producers of this book wish to express their recognition to the following people and institutions, without whose support this book would have never been possible: to the Consejo Nacional para la Cultura y las Artes, to the Instituto Nacional de Antropología e Historia and to the Instituto de Cultura de Tabasco, for having granted us the permits necessary to photograph and reproduce the figurines in the collections of museums under them. To Editorial Raíces and *Arqueología Mexicana* for having allowed the reproduction of pieces in the Museo Nacional de Antropología. Our special acknowledgment goes to Rogelio Vergara for his help with the texts.

To Don José Aguilar, Director of the Museo Regional de Campeche, whose exemplary enthusiasm and dedication allowed us to photograph the pieces at the Museum he heads, those in a temporary exhibit at the Museo del Fuerte de San Miguel (*Ciudades Mayas* temporary exhibition) and those in the Museo del Camino Real de Hecelchakán; to the I.N.A.H. guards at Jaina island; to Mr. Osvaldo Chan, who is in charge of the Museo del Camino Real de Hecelchakán; to the personnel at the Museo de Balancán, Tabasco; to Archaeologist Arnoldo González Cruz, Director of the Palenque Archaeological Site; to the Museography personnel at the Museo de Sitio de Palenque, who enthusiastically supported our efforts despite the ungodly hours at which we were working; to Professor Omar Huerta Escalante, Director of the Museo de Jonuta, in Tabasco, who gave us help beyond what would have been expectable for the purpose of overcoming serious logistical disadvantages when we photographed at the museum he heads; to Doctor Charles Spencer, curator of the Hall of Mexico and Central America at the American Museum of Natural History; to Dr. Steve Whittington, Director of the University of Maine's Hudson Museum; to Nancy Rosoff, assistant curator at the National Museum of the American Indian <Research Branch> (Smithsonian Institution); to Dr. Susan Matheson, Director of the Yale University Art Gallery and to Dr. Mary Ellen Miller, Chairperson of the Art History Department at that same University, who was crucial in our success to secure the necessary photography permits at the Art Gallery; to Professor Gillett Griffin, Curator of the Mesoamerican Art Hall at Princeton University's Art Museum, who was always fully behind us and ready with encouragement during our work there; and, last but not least, to Deborah Windero, who obtained the permits we requested and assisted us while we worked at the Munson-Williams-Proctor Institute.

Finally, special recognition must go to Beatrice Koch, of New York City, without whose generous help and support at a critical stage in our project, this book would have never materialized.

PRESENTATION

A soil of fragmented shells and sand, covered with layers of lime-rich earth, a mangrove barrier, supported by stilt-like floating roots and a wide variety of coastal birds formed the environment in which the settlement of Jaina, off the Campeche coast, was founded.

Two branches of the lower Usumacinta river that form the island of Chinal, an enormous artificial platform and surrounding savannas and swamps with interspersed tropical forest spots were the components among which the settlement of Jonuta, Tabasco took place.

And steep, rocky foothills, a tall tropical forest and a varied jungle fauna that includes the growls of howler monkeys served as the backdrop for the development of the city of Palenque, Chiapas.

These three pre-Columbian centers in the Maya region were not the only ones in which terracotta figurines were made. Other sites include Altar de Sacrificios, Comalcalco, Los Guarixés and Uaymil. Nevertheless, Jaina, Jonuta and Palenque are so well-known and have produced so many pieces that they can very well be used for a study of this tradition.

The expressive figurines found in Jaina, Jonuta and Palenque are veritable small-scale clay sculptures, mainly used to accompany the dead in their final journey. In a way, these figurines also died. When dug up by archaeologists, however, they are reborn and claim a place as memorable beings of their time.

These delicate sculptures bear no names, but are rich in gestures and expressions; they are the hidden faces of anonymous people, faithfully rendered by nameless artists, who conscientiously copied every detail of the clothing and the finery of their models, the marks of their social rank and the daily scenes of their communities.

Executed with great mastery and realism, they often doubled as whistles and rattles, though they were probably not used as musical instruments in mundane festivities, but rather in special religious festivals. We do not know whether they were made as trade objects, esteemed only because of their aesthetic value or whether they were part of the cult of ancestors and death.

This last proposition seems to be the most plausible one. A family could have acquired the figurine of a ballplayer if one of its members had been a ballplayer; they could also commission one especially if someone in the household practiced the game. Thus, a figurine could become an object of family veneration that could even be used to accompany the deceased in their long journey to the Underworld.

Figurines could be made through different methods: modeling the clay by hand, using molds to shape it and, sometimes, by combining both techniques. The clay, without a de-greasing agent, was preferably orange and sometimes tan; modeled figurines are more abundant, perhaps due to a greater demand for them. It is very common to find on them the vestiges of white, red and blue paint, the symbolism of which might be related to the North and death (white), the East and life (red) and the world of the holy (blue).

The vast corpus of figurines known represents humans, animals and deities; among the first ones, there are all kinds of people and everyday scenes (one of the preferred themes of the sculptors-potters that created them). Among the representations of animals, some are very realistic renderings of their subjects, while others are more fantastic and may point towards religious concepts.

In general, figurines are part of a common cultural tradition, as is the custom of perpetuating human life after death; however, they are also a reflection of the group that produced them, something that allows us to detect variations in the physical type of a region's figurines, as opposed to those produced elsewhere.

Thus, the physical types of Jaina, Jonuta and Palenque are alike and different at the same time. They share a resemblance in their general features, but differ in the details; this may be explained by the fact that the people from Jaina were essentially Yucatec Maya, those from Jonuta were Chontal, while those from Palenque were Chol; all derive from a single, very ancient ethnical and linguistic trunk and all settled the same geographical area and interacted among themselves.

Among the shared physical features are low to medium height, stocky bodies, dark skin, straight, black hair, slanted eyes, due to the epicanthic fold and high cheekbones; differences can be found in the shape of the nose, due to cranial deformation, which led to the almost complete disappearance of the nose bridge and its smooth merging into the forehead, as well as other artificially created beauty traits, such as strabismus, scarification and dental mutilation.

Figurine portraits reveal several traits of ancient Maya society. In the socio-political pyramid, we have the supreme lord of a site: the *ah pop* or *ahaw*, who carries the richest clothing imaginable: a woven skirt, held in place by a broad sash with a pleated front end and a long rear one (often doubling as a stand for figurines), rich necklaces made with large jade beads (sometimes forming veritable capes and aprons), helmet-like headdresses, festooned with long feathers and flowers, high-ankle leather sandals, anklets and wristlets, large jade earflares and scarification designs from the corners of the mouth to the cheeks.

The rank immediately below these high lords often ruled subsidiary sites. Overseen by an *ah pop* (he of the mat), they were known as *halach uinic* (true man) and rivaled their masters in their use of finery: animal-head helmets, feathers, mantles and aprons adorned with countless motifs, skirts, belts, sandals, loincloths, wristlets, earflares, fans and wooden stools.

Next in rank were the *batab* or district lords, who donned less luxurious clothing, followed by the warlords, who often wore headgear with the heads of animals, feathered headdresses, bucal masks, tunics and special cotton armor, wristlets, sandals and rectangular shields. Their hair was normally long, tied in a ponytail and sometimes painted, as was the face. Body paint was used to enhance an appearance of fierceness.

Priests played an important role in Maya society and religious officials are present in the figurines. Their main characteristics are the use of loincloths, long shirts or mantles folded towards the front, shell pectorals hanging from the neck, hair gathered on top of the head, jade-disc diadems, arms crossed over the chest and cheek scarification (from eye to chin) with symmetrical designs. Some seem to indicate the deity they were affiliated to, as in the case of those who have two concentric circles around one eye and a half skin mask relating them to the god of commerce, war and human sacrifice.

In Maya society there were merchants who carried wares from one region to another as well as different craftsmen and artists, such as dancers, musicians, painters, ballplayers, dwarfs or actors.

Ballplayers represented in the figurines either adopt dynamic postures, or else stand or sit. They are often depicted kneeling on one knee (protected by a special kneepad), folding their left arm, which is also protected by a cotton wrapping and with their waist protected by a broad, padded sash, sometimes made of separate parts and kept in place by a belt. In other cases, they wear so-called *yokes* to protect the abdominal area and, in general, they wear a wristlet on their right arm.

Male representations include dwarfs, who were related to the supernatural and the world of the dead. Because of this, they accompanied both lords and ballplayers, aiding and serving them to bring them luck and well-being. We also find figurines of hunchbacks, sick and deformed people. Among the dwarfs, there is a fat character, wearing a full-body feather suit, who brings to mind the so-called "Fat God" of the coastal area, probably related to abundance.

There are also men in disguise as either real or fantastic animals, who could have been participants in certain festivities; old men embracing young women; young and old people emerging from flowers and even men with human skin masks, torn from sacrificed captives, covering their cheeks and chin and probably relating them with the Spring god Xipe.

Important women display the clothes and jewelry that mark their high status; some braid their hair, while others gather it in a bun on top of their heads; some display facial decoration; many wear long skirts and blouses, sandals, necklaces, earflares and, sometimes, fans or hats.

There are women with short-sleeved, long *huipiles* , wristlets, earplugs and spindles with thread in their hands; perhaps they are priestesses for the goddess of weaving, Ix Chel or Ix Chebel Yax; we also find weavers, sometimes accompanied by parrots sitting in front of tree stumps to which they have tied their waist looms.

Women may dress with a skirt held in place by a woven sash with an undulating band that ends with *tau*-shaped wind symbols, pronounced *ik'* in Mayan. Over the long skirt, they wear long-sleeved *huipiles*, ending with jaguar-shaped designs, from the open mouth of which protrude *ik'*- shaped tongues. Besides earflares and necklace, they often carry fans and elaborate headdresses.

There are also blind women and women in humble clothes; old, seated women with a piece of fabric folded on top of one knee, pregnant women, women who nurse or carry their babies. There is also a variety of hollow figurines, made of a fine orange clay and often painted in white, who raise either one or both arms, showing the palms of the hands and wearing clothes with designs that are very similar to those found in Central Veracruz.

There are some who have mobile limbs. These may have been used as puppets or in special representations. They remind one of the Teotihuacan and Gulf Coast figurines.

Regarding the images of animals, we find much of the fauna that inhabited the region: owls, wild turkeys, macaws, parrots, pelicans, ducks and buzzards, as well as jaguars, rabbits, monkeys, armadillos, snakes, crocodiles, turtles and dogs. Most of these figurines were built as whistles.

Many objects can be identified on figurines: fans, hats, stools, benches, shields, masks, headdresses with animal heads, flowers, feathers, earflares, necklaces, wristlets, pectorals, sandals, musical instruments, waist looms and skirts, *huipiles*, tunics, sashes, loincloths, belts, capes, etc.

We can identify the materials with which these objects were made: palm leaf, cotton, wood, animal skins, jade, bone, shell, conch, turtle shell, rubber, pigments, clay, etc. We also gain an insight into the crafts involved in making them: spinning, weaving and dyeing of clothes, mat and hat weaving, tanning, stoneworking, woodcarving, pottery, carpentry and more.

Chronologically, solid figurines seem to belong to an older tradition, perhaps stemming from the Medium Classic period (between 500 and 600 A.D.), while hollow mold figurines may correspond to a different, Late Classic to Epiclassic period tradition (between 600 and 1000 A.D.).

They are extraordinary because of their faithfulness to their human models and the perfection of their execution; they are also surprising, as they afford us a rare glimpse of the aristocratic postures and gestures of the nobility, the fierce countenance of warriors, the pathetic helplessness and sadness of sick, blind and old people, the strength of ballplayers, the calm demeanor of weavers, the devotion of religious officials and the myriad other emotions that can be readily guessed in those faces, that have truly returned from the Underworld.

This is what the reader will find in this book, as he / she contemplates the splendid illustrations of a vast gallery of figurines from the collections of several major museums.

Román Piña Chan
Chimaliztac, Spring 1997

A WINDOW
INTO ANOTHER WORLD

To David Schele,
my beloved husband,
for all the love and patience he showed for a lifetime.

Early in my career I attended the International Congress of Americanists, a meeting that was held in the Museo Nacional de Antropología in Mexico City in 1974. At the time, a Chinese art exhibition that included the recently discovered jade suits of an ancient king and his consort was on display in the same museum. Since it was a unique opportunity, I spent each noon break in the meeting during the week going through one or two rooms of that exhibition instead of eating lunch. Toward the end of the week, I arranged to meet a friend in the Maya room of the museum so that we could check an inscription together. It so happened that this was also the day I spent with the Tang horses and other clay images of lords and ladies wrought by great Chinese artists. While I waited for my friend, I decided to look at the figurines from the island of Jaina.

I remember being struck by the contrast. The Maya figurines were not nearly as sophisticated technologically. They were not high fired nor did they have glazes, and generally they were smaller than their Chinese counterparts. Yet with all the fame accorded to the Tang horses and other imagery modeled by Chinese artists, I felt a liveliness in the Maya figurines that was missing in the Chinese art.

The Maya figurines represented individual people who had readable expressions on their faces. Their bodies were caught in the middle of actions and the people who had made them paid attention to the smallest detail to show how their clothes were made. There was an energy about these figurines that lent them life, and I knew that they opened a window into what it was to live in Maya society thirteen-hundred years ago.

I had been drawn to Maya figurines in the first place through the photography of Irmgard Groth and others who published figurine collections in the 1960s. I had made slides of those photographs early in my career and used them in teaching to help my students train their imaginations about how the ancient Maya looked. When I had a chance to work with Jorge Pérez de Lara to create a new book on Maya figurines, I jumped at it because it gave me an opportunity to indulge an old love of mine. My hope is that this book will ignite the imaginations of many other people so that they will be able to see the ancient Maya in the mind's eye as I have done.

The imagery in these elegant figurines is not unique. They capture activities and show people and things that also appear on the carved stone monuments of the Classic period, but they are different in very important ways. For example, we see far more women in the figurines than we do in the monumental imagery. Just as important is the three-dimensional form of the figurines. We can turn them to find out how things appeared from the sides and back. The clay artists showed us how the Maya fastened on their clothes and how the headdresses worked. This detail enriches our understanding of the flat drawings on stelae or in pottery paintings in ways that cannot be matched by any other media.

The making of figurines began in Mesoamerica by the Early Formative period (1500 B.C.). Figurines from this early period usually have slit eyes and punctated pupils, but artists from the most famous sites of Tlatilco, Xochipala, and Las Bocas could model figures in powerfully naturalistic styles. The Olmec especially favored life-sized hollow figurines representing babies in various positions and pottery modeled into the forms of animals. Many are exceptionally life-like in their representation. Hollow figurines in the Olmec-style also depicted lords dressed in the regalia of power and authority as they engaged in rituals of various sorts.

The solid clay figurines from the Valley of Xochipala belong to one of the most extraordinary traditions in Mesoamerica. Although Xochipala figurines are usually small (from 10 cm up to 25 cm) they display an astonishingly detailed anatomy. Tiny toes and exquisitely modeled fingers grace minuscule feet and hands, while miniature faces complete with teeth and pupils in the eyes depict clearly readable emotions.

Other early traditions were more schematic in their representations of human beings. Tlatilco figurines present generalized bodies and faces that do not attempt to reproduce people in a naturalistic manner. Especially in representations of women, hips and legs are much larger in proportion to the body

than in life and the artists did not attempt to capture the impression of individual people.

Eastern Mesoamerica and the Maya region also produced early figurine traditions that, like the Tlatilco one, used generalized features and made no attempt to distinguish one individual from another. Formative-period (Preclassic in the nomenclature of the Maya region) figurines are usually found only as broken heads, but they are always recognizable because of the style of the eyes. They have drilled pupils in the middle of ridged slits.

The Classic period saw an elaboration of the figurine tradition throughout Mesoamerica. By A.D. 100, Teotihuacan was making thousands of solid-core figures, often representing women in their *huipils* and with turban-like headdresses. By A.D. 450, the repertoire of figurines expanded to include representations of warriors, rulers, symbols of war, etc. Moreover, some of the imagery is rare or unknown in Teotihuacan painting so that important iconography and symbolism resided only in the figurines. Teotihuacan also developed a tradition of censers carved in an extraordinary style that adds yet other images and symbols to Teotihuacan's symbolic language. Large hollow figurines holding arrays of smaller solid core figurines became an important ritual assemblage during this later period of Teotihuacan's history.

The Teotihuacan traditions of clay modeling and pottery painting seem to have been one of the principal vehicles that carried Teotihuacan symbolism to the rest of Mesoamerica. During the Early Classic period, the people living in the Escuintla province of southern Guatemala developed a style of censers clearly derived from the Teotihuacan tradition, although there were differences in the symbols they attached to them. The Teotihuacan symbols and images that appeared suddenly in the Early Classic art from the Maya lowlands come primarily from Teotihuacan figurines rather than from the paintings of that distant city. These Teotihuacan traits include the balloon and bird headdresses, the Mosaic War Serpent headdress, the square shields with a goggle-eyed deity, and the war symbol of a super-imposed owl, crossed spears, and a shield with a hand. Although Teotihuacan-style figurines have been rarely found in archaeological contexts in the Maya zone, the fact that the critical imagery occurs mostly on figurines suggests that they provided a crucial medium for the exchange of ideas and symbols. They have advantages in this role: they are portable and they are three-dimensional.

The Maya of the southern lowlands amplified their own earlier traditions of figurines and censers simultaneously to the Teotihuacanos. Unfortunately, the Early Classic portions of those traditions are not well known because archaeologists know less about that period. Excavators found solid-core figurines at Río Azul and a large hollow one at Yaxuná in northern Yucatán, but large modeled censers and carved cache vessels in the form of buckets and plates were far more popular in the Petén and Belize than figurines. Those early figurines we have include modeled representations of rulers or gods seated on thrones. Many of these broke apart like cookie jars to allow offerings to be placed inside or incense to be burned in the bottom buckets. We know "cookie-jar" figurines and censers ranging from small to large (up to a meter in height) from Kaminaljuyú, Copán, Tikal, and Waxaktun. An archaeologist also found a Teotihuacan-style hollow figurine with interior solid figures atop the collapsed ruins of a palace at Becán. Unfortunately, the zone in which the figurine traditions are the strongest (northern Chiapas, Tabasco, and Campeche) has not been the focus of deep excavations designed to discover Early Classic architecture and associated burials and caches. Thus, the apparent predominance of Late Classic figurines may well be the result of a bias in the archaeological record.

Late Classic figurines are known from Waxaktun, Tikal, Alta Verapaz, Chamá, Lubaantún, Piedras Negras, Yaxchilán, Lagartero, and many other sites, but by far and away, the most developed tradition of Maya figurines occurred in the western area. I have often wondered if this focus on figurines may have come from the relatively low development of narrative pottery painting in the same western zone. I have noticed that many of the same characters and actions shown on the narrative pottery from Petén cities show up in the figurine traditions of the western cities.

The Maya made their figurines in several ways. They could be modeled individually by hand or created entirely or partially from molds. The molds we have are made of fired clay into which wet clay was pressed. The backs of these press-mold figurines were completed by hand. Sometimes the head was made from molds and designed with a tenon to insert into a separately made body. Sculptors added details to both hand-made and mold-made figurines using an *appliqué* technique. Hand-made figurines often had their clothes added in individual layers. This tells us a great deal about how clothes and other accouterments were made.

The potters used clays of many different colors, often tempered with fairly coarse material, to make their figurines. Apparently the Maya fired them in open kilns that often left blackened burn marks where wood touched the clay. They often painted the finished figurines with bright colors to add verisimilitude. Figurines could be made from solid clay, but because many of them were hollow, they have holes to let the expanding gases escape during firing. Figurines could simply represent people, gods, and animals without any other function, but the potters often made the hollow figurines into rattles, whistles, or flutes to be used in ritual. Both figurines and whistles were pierced so that they could be worn as pendants.[1]

The most famous of all sources for figurines is the island of Jaina just off the west coast of Campeche. This island had residential areas complete with pyramids and plazas, but many archaeologists have suggested that it was a burial ground for towns and cities located nearby on the mainland. Jaina has been known since the nineteenth century when Charnay visited and excavated some of the mounds. Archaeologists from the Mexican Instituto Nacional de Antropología e Historia have excavated there in 1940-1942, 1945, 1947, 1957, and 1964. The majority of the figurines in the museums of Mexico come from these excavations.[2]

Most of the figurines from Jaina Island come from graves so that they seem to be intended to accompany the dead into the Afterlife. This may account for the repetition of similar figurines in many different graves. The same kind of offering would be efficacious for the dead of many different families. Román Piña Chan, who excavated many of the figurines, said that families dressed their dead in their best clothing, put a jade bead in their mouth, placed personal adornments and possessions around their bodies, and set figurines in their arms before wrapping the body up in a bundle of cotton cloth and mats. The families tied adults into either a flexed or a fetal position for their burials, while they placed the bundles containing children inside large vases before interment.

After placing the burial bundle of adults in a grave lying on their backs or on a side, the family sprinkled cinnabar or hematite over the bundle, set a plate over the head, and laid offerings around the body. The offerings consisted of vessels, figurines, ornaments of stone and shell, artifacts of obsidian and other materials, whistles, flutes, and finally food and drink for the journey to the Otherworld. Pit graves for interring the vessels containing dead children were usually no more than a meter deep.

Using these burial patterns, Román Piña Chan deduced Maya beliefs about death and the afterlife. He noted that the people of Jaina and most other sites sent their dead on the journey after life with food and drink, their possessions and tools for work, and with their best clothes and jewelry so that life after death must have resembled the life they had known before death. The fetal position he interpreted as a reference to an expected rebirth. Subsequent research into the symbolism of death, rebirth, and Creation have confirmed his ideas concerning Maya expectations about death and the afterlife.

The great majority of figurines from Jaina and elsewhere simply show men or women dressed in the regalia of their lives and offices. Perhaps the Maya sent these images into the Otherworld with their dead so that the soul would understand its role and responsibility among the ancestral dead. Other figurines depicting gods or *nawals* may also have evoked help for the soul in its journey through Xibalbá to become an ancestor.

However, not all figurines were intended for use by the dead. I learned this during my many years working at Palenque during the decade of the seventies. While cataloging the storehouse of excavated material at the site, Peter Mathews and I found large cans full of figurine heads and body parts that had been excavated from the rubble, offerings, and tombs all over the site. Moreover, when I took walks in the forest around Palenque between 1970 and 1975, I found many figurine heads and body parts lying around on the ground and among the fallen stones of collapsed buildings. In fact, every time there was a thunder storm, more fragments washed out of the hillsides onto the forest floors.

I also saw thick deposits of figurine parts peaking out from the debris that had been thrown off the back of residential platforms. At least one of the zones had molds among the debris so that figurines may have been made by the residents of that compound. Great garbage deposits of broken figurines have been found by Suzanna Eckholm at Lagartero, a site in southern Chiapas. Like the Palenque figurines, the Lagartero hoards represent humans, animals, *nawals*, and gods. Many are in the form of whistles, but Eckholm also identified a set of them as pendants to be worn. Some of the figurines from elsewhere may also have served as parts of clothing.

Although little has been published about Palenque's figurine tradition, I can attest that the people of Palenque used figurines in religious rituals involving both their temples and their homes. Perhaps children also played with figurines, but I suspect figurines more likely served the same purpose as figures of the *santos* do today in Maya towns and homes. Most of the figurine heads I have seen represent beautifully modelled humans, but I have also seen the heads of gods, heroes, *nawals*, and many of the creatures that appear in the narratives on the painted pottery from Petén cities. Since the figurines also come from caches and tombs, it may be that the people of Palenque and other western cities like Jonuta and Comalcalco used figurines to construct three-dimensional narrative scenes recording events from their daily lives and from the stories of *nawals* and gods that lay at the heart of their religion. Assemblages of figurines such as I propose are known from Postclassic contexts at Santa Rita, Belize.

Finally, Stephen Houston and David Stuart have contributed a new interpretation from the hieroglyphic inscriptions that may explain one way that the ancient Maya used their figurines, censers, and other imagery in their temples, their homes, and their graves. When the Maya carved an image of a historical person or showed a person dressed as a god, they often placed a text next to it to identify who was shown. These texts always begin with the same glyph. For decades we have known it reads *u bah*, but we thought it was a general verb of some sort (something like "he is"). Houston and Stuart have pointed out that *bah* means "likeness, same as, similar to" in Yukatek, while in Chortí, it means "body, self, a being, a spirit".

According to the proposed interpretation, images are more than just similarities or likenesses, but rather they are people or beings portrayed complete with their "self-ness" and spiritual essence. Today, the Maya of highland Guatemala hold exactly this concept about their *santos* and sacred stones called *q'abawil*. This word, *q'abawil*, means "a statue, a sacred image, a saint, and the spirit that inhabits a saint." It is not just to be difficult that the Tzotzil Maya of San Juan Chamula do not let outsiders take photographs of their saints, but because they believe the image in a photograph is the same as the saint. It must be honored and protected in the same way.

If the concept of *bah* is a manifestation of self and spirit that transfers into an image, then the figurines are the *bah* of the people, gods, and spirits they represent. They are not dolls or playthings for children. Instead they functioned as material embodiments for the spirit selves of people and supernaturals in rituals and offerings and for sending with the dead into the Otherworld. Once the figurine had been broken or the likeness in a sculpture effaced, then the *bah* or self would no longer reside in the object. This concept accounts for the well-documented practice of killing objects, carried out by the Maya for centuries.

Linda Schele
Austin, Winter 1996

---

[1] SUSANNA ECKHOLM (1985) made this suggestion considering a group of figurines she excavated at Lagartero, and Rands and Rands (1973) identified the practice with whistle-type figurines.

[2] ROMÁN PIÑA-CHAN, (*Jaina la casa en el agua,* 1968) described these excavations and provided the principal information we now have on the archaeological context of Jaina figurines.

WOMEN, WEAVERS
AND MIDWIVES

Women played an important role in the Maya creation myth and in society and the family. Their foremost role was, of course, that of mother, wife, and house keeper. They prepared food and raised children, and held important political positions as the primary caretakers and early educators of heirs. For the nobility, marriage was an instrument of alliance and affiliation. Nobles and kings married more than one woman in order to create and maintain networks of political and familial ties. The Maya recorded these important affiliations through parentage statements and titles that often referred to the woman's original home. All of the data we have gathered from these parentage statements and name patterns suggest that the Classic Maya used a patrilineal kinship system, so that the offspring belonged to the family of the father. It was a matter of intense political importance which of a royal man's offspring became his heir, because he could have children by several women. Not only did the status of royal wife bring important affiliations and opportunities to the male relatives of a woman, but if her child became the heir and next king, the family of the mother gained special access to political power and wealth.

The inscriptional histories name most women because of their roles as wives of the kings and mothers of the heirs, but scribes rarely recorded them as the protagonists of actions. Nevertheless, women played important political roles in the lives of their sons and husbands. At Piedras Negras, women appear in the stelae

recording the accessions of kings, although we do not know if they were the mothers or the wives of the kings. At Palenque, the mother of the king gave him the *tok'-pakal*, "flint-shield", symbol of war during the latter's accession rites. At Yaxchilan, the wife of Itzam-Balam let blood from her tongue to conjure up Yat-Balam, the founder of Yaxchilan's dynasty, during her husband's accession rites. On Lintel 25, the founder's image carrying the shield and spear of war, the *tok'-pakal*, emerges from the great War Serpent called Waxaklahun-Ubah-Kan. In the Bonampak' murals and on Stela 2, both mother and wife of the king appear in all the important rituals he chose to memorialize with imagery (including the torture and disposal of captives he had taken in battle).

The inscriptions record many women, but some of them were more famous and powerful than others. For example, Lady Olnal, the ninth person to rule Palenque, was the only woman ever to have ruled a Maya city in her own right (at least according to the inscriptions). Another famous woman sealed a dynastic break at Naranjo that had been caused by war with Caracol. She was Lady Kan-Ahaw-Tzuk, the daughter of king Balah-Kan-K'awil of Dos Pilas, who sent his daughter to marry a noble of Naranjo. The offspring of that marriage, Tiliw-Kan-Chak, led Naranjo back to its former glory.

Finally, the most honored woman in Maya history was Lady K'abal-Xok of Yaxchilan. She was the principal wife of Itzam-Balam, who married another, younger woman from Kalak'mul

Plate 1 (20.8 cm) Museo Nacional de Antropología. INAH/RAICES.

Plate 2 (18.2 cm) American Museum of Natural History N.W.C. Collections Management Fund (44002110).

Plate 3 (20.3 cm) American Museum of Natural History N.W.C. Collections Management Fund (44002110).

late in his life. The son of that later marriage, Yaxun-Balam, eventually succeeded his father, but only after ten years of conflict. Itzam-Balam tried to ease the resistance of the local lineages to the child of the foreign marriage by constructing Temple 23 with three of the most magnificent lintels ever commissioned by a Maya ruler. Lady K'abal-Xok and her kinsmen lost their battle against that foreign wife and her offspring, but she won the war of history. Her images grace the British Museum and the Museo Nacional de Antropología e Historia so that she has become the model of ancient Maya womanhood.

Women had their roles in the divine world as well. In the story of Creation, the Moon Goddess in both an old and young form played critical roles in the Fourth Creation. The Old Moon Goddess called Chak-Chel, "Great (or Red) Rainbow," was the midwife of Creation who enabled the rebirth of the Maize God and the birth of his sons. Shown as a toothless old woman with sunken breasts, she cares for children, weaves with exacting mastery, and in the Dresden Codex, she poured water from her vase as he helped God L, Ek'-Chuwah, create the flood that destroyed the Third Creation.

Plate 4 (17.4 cm) Museo Regional de Campeche. INAH.

The Young Moon Goddess was also a weaver, but she was always shown as a beautiful young woman of child-bearing age. In fact, the glyph representing her head became the glyph for the number one, *hun*, and for "lady", sometimes read as *Na'*, "mother" and "noble lady" and sometimes read as *Ixik*, "lady". Sculptors represented the mothers and wives of kings as the Moon Goddess so that she became the model of all womanhood. In the Dresden Codex, she carried the name Uh-Ixik, "Moon Lady", and Sak-Ixik, "White or Weaver Lady", while in the Classic inscriptions, she was Ixik Uh, "Lady Moon", and Na-Huntan, "Lady Caretaker". The Moon Goddess was the mother of the Hero Twins, Hun-Ahaw and Yax-Balam, and like her old counterpart, Chak-Chel, she was a weaver. As Ixik Sak (written with the head variant that is both the number two and the color white), she attended God L in his house.

Another goddess named Na-Kolel (Lady Homemaker) greeted an old deer god as he emerged from a serpent and she attended him in death. Most important are the goddesses (usually unnamed) who attend and dress the newly reborn Maize God just before the Fourth Creation was realized. They can be shown nude or half-dressed as they tie on his jewelry and apply the face paint that brings him finally to life. A Maya woman from Rabinal in Guatemala told me that her father asked her to walk with him among the growing corn in the fam-

22

Plate 5 ´23.5 cm) Museo Nacional de Antropclogía. INAH.

ily milpa because while men can plant the corn, only women can give it the kind of nurturing that will make it strong and abundant.

The Maya portrayed women in figurines far more frequently than in any other artistic medium they used. We cannot tell if the female figurines depicted goddesses in one of their many aspects or if they show women in their lives as wives, mothers, and members of the court. I suspect that mos: of them represented historical women or the idea of "woman", but for historical women, the concepts of the Moon Goddess as mother and nurturer lay at the heart of being a woman and the way the Maya represented women both in figurines and in stone sculpture.

These figurines (plates 1-6) depict women dressed in their finest clothes standing in the formal position they used in ritual contexts. Their clothing consists of two parts (an underskirt called a *pik* in the lowland languages like Yucatec and Chol and an *uq* in highland languages like K'iche). Made of wide strips of cloth sewn together along the side seams, the *pik* covered the body from just under the bosom to the ankles. Pictures of the *pikob* (the suffix *-ob* forms the plural of words in Mayan) in the Dresden Codex show them with shoulder straps, but these do not appear on figurines from the Classic period. Weavers often wove colorful patterns into the fabric of the *pik*, especially along the lower border.

Plate 6 (15.8 cm) Museo del Camino Real de Hekelchak'an. INAH.

Over the *pik*, women wore a *k'ub*, an overblouse today called a *huipil* after the Aztec name for this garment. In the highlands of Guatemala, *po't* is the word for this overblouse. Once again the *k'ub* consisted of woven strips sewn together, probably along a center in the front and back, and at the edges to make a pseudo-sleeve that covered the upper arms. All these figurines show forearms, wrists, and hands emerging from the sleeves. Most carry objects including, a round mirror, a small bag, a fan, a bag made of twisted fabric, and a string of large beads.

Women wore their hair long, but with their faces framed by locks cut into a stepped arrangement also worn by men. They wound decorated bands of various widths around the rest of their long hair, arranging the bound locks into high elaborate patterns. They tied wider headbands around their heads to hold up the elaborate hair arrangements and often set flowers into the hairdos. Today Maya women in the Guatemalan highlands still use gorgeously woven hair bands to create equally elaborate hairdos, each associated with a particular town and tradition.

The *k'ubob* worn by Maya women had several different forms. Some had round or square neck openings only large enough for

Plate 7 (19.3 cm) Museo Nacional de Antropología. INAH/RAICES.

Plate 8 (12.8 cm) Museo del Camino Real de Hekelchak'an. INAH.

Plate 9 (22.5 cm) Museo Regional de Campeche. INAH.

the head to pass through. Other *k'ub* openings were large enough for the shoulders to pass through, so that the *k'ub* rested on the upper arms. Some *k'ubob* were short, while others fell below the knees. Some were plain weave, but many displayed elaborate, colorful patterns that covered the entire surface of the blouse. *K'ub* patterns often played against those woven into the *pik* under them. The cloth woven with the fine net pattern we see in one figurine (plate 7) was transparent so that the woman's breasts were visible through the cloth. Maya painters captured this transparency in several pottery scenes.

Women often wore single and multiple-stranded necklaces made of jade, other precious stones, and shells worked into beads of various shapes. The women on the figurines (plates 7-12) wear relatively simple necklaces, while the high-ranked women depicted on stone monuments often wore jade capes as well as necklaces. Ear ornaments could also be made of jade, other stones, or shell, and were often shaped to represent flowers. The word for "collar" or "necklace" was *uh*; "earflares" were *tup*, and the precious stones and other materials used to make jewelry were *k'an*. In these and other figurines,

Plate 10 (16.8 cm) Museo del Camino Real de Hekelchak'an. INAH.

blue marked the jades and was a favorite color of cloth.

Women could also go through their day wearing only their *pik*. Many figurines show women with bare breasts as they carry on conversations and participate in their daily lives. Today in the back country of Guatemala and Chiapas, women still work through the heat of the day wearing only their skirts. Exposing their breasts by wearing only their *pik* or by

wearing a transparent *k'ub* was not a violation of modesty to the ancient Maya.

The blue paint on the two seated figurines (plates 13 and 14) may signal the presence of one of these transparent blouses or the possibility of body paint as a part of Maya decoration for ritual performance. The small standing figurine from Jonuta (plate 16) shows a smiling woman wearing a wrap-around skirt that barely covers her breasts. Today Maya

Plate 11 ̄17 cm) Museo Nacional de Antropología. INAH.

Plate 12 (14.3 cm) Museo de Jonuta. Instituto de Cultura del Estado de Tabasco.

Plate 13 (22.4 cm) The Art Museum, Princeton University. Gift of Gillett G. Griffin.

Plate 14 15.3 cm) Museo Nacional de Antropología. INAH.

women in the highlands were ɫ *ikob* very much like this.

Nude figurines are almost unknown, although naked ladies help dress the Maize God after he was reborn in the Ballcourt of Xibalba. One figurine in this group (plate 15) depicts a lady wearing only a belt, a necklace, and her wristlets, as she cocks her head to the side with her long, unbound hair falling in front of her shoulder. The sculptor depicted full anatomical detail in the front and the creases in her wide buttocks behind. She holds her hands in front of her body in some un-known action. We do not know if she was bathing, perhaps washing clothes, or engaged in a ritual. If she represents a scene from myth, perhaps she is one of the goddess who redressed the Maize God and helped him back to life.

Women like men could wear elaborate headdresses signalling their status, affiliation, rank, name, and deity associations. The seated lady in this group (plate 17) wears a wrapped headdress made of long, elaborately tied ribbons. Headdresses of this type appear on ballplayers and other male lords in the imag-

31

Plate 15 (22.8 cm) Yale University Art Gallery, Gift of the Olsen Foundation.

Plate 16 (16.6 cm. Museo de Jonuta. Instituto de Cultura del Estado de Tabasco.

Plate 17 (19.5 cm) The Art Museum, Princeton University. Gift of J. Lionberger Davis.

ery of Chich'en Itza. The word for headdress or headband was *hun* or *hunal*, while a headwrap was *pixom*.

One standing woman (plate 18) wears a headdress featuring an arch of feathers and a diving bird atop her head. A similar diving bird appears in a woman's headdress on the side of Tikal Stela 25, so that this Jonuta lady wears symbolism that was shared by her Tikal counterparts. The pregnant woman (plate 19)

holds her long hair in one hand as she stands wearing only her *pik* and a belt, which were called *t'et'*, *xok*, *wit'*, or *xechel pik* in Yucatec, and *yit nak* or *k'ab* in Chorti.

The next group of figurines (plates 20-24), most of them from Jonuta, show the role of women as the caretakers of children and animals. Four of them (plates 20-23) depict children with their mothers who have their breasts bare for nursing. Most are dressed in

Plate 18 (23 cm) Museo de Jonuta. Instituto de Cultura del Estado de Tabasco.

Plate 19 (17.3 cm) Museo Nacional de Antropología. INAH/RAICES.

Plate 20 (17.8 cm) Yale University Art Gallery, Gift of the Olsen Foundation.

Plate 21 (10.7 cm. Museo de Jonuta. Instituto de Cultura del Estado de Tabasco.

elaborate headgear and appear to be going about their business taking their children with them just as modern Maya women do. Mayan languages have different words for "child", depending on whether one is referring to the mother or father. In Yucatec, *al* was "child of woman", while *mehen* was the "child of man". *Almehen* was a word for "noble" because they were descended from nobility through both parents. These children are all *al*, but they may also have been *almehenob*.

One woman holds the head of a child with a deer headdress in her lap (plate 23), although the body of the child is not visible. Perhaps the image represents a sleeping child who has worked his way under her *pik*. The deer may represent the child's name or his animal spirit companion. Another figurine from Jonuta (plate 24) depicts an older woman with an elaborately woven *k'ub* holding a dog in her arm. Dogs and turkeys lived with human beings, although the Maya did

37

Plate 22 (18.4 cm) Museo de Jonuta. Instituto de Cultura del Estado de Tabasco.

not treat dogs as pets. Dogs scavenged for food and very likely helped clean up human waste from the households in which they lived. Today in Yucatan, both pigs and dogs perform the same function. The Maya also ate their dogs and their turkeys. Dog is *pek* in Yucatec and *tz'i* in most other Mayan languages.

Weaving, one of the principal activities of women, was a source of wealth for the Maya. It was collected as tribute and given out as gifts from rulers to subordinates. As impor-

Plate 23 (17.1 cm) Museo de Jonuta. Instituto de Cultura del Estado de Tabasco.

Plate 24 (22.5 cm) Museo de Jonuta. Instituto de Cultura del Estado de Tabasco.

Plate 25 (16.5 cm) Museo Nacional de Antropología. INAH/RAICES.

tant, weaving and the work of weavers provided some of the central metaphors for order and creation.

In Yucatec *sak* is "weave" and the name of the prototypical weaver, the moon goddess was Sak Ixik, "White Woman" or "Weaving Woman". In the Cholan languages, *hal*, the verb for "to weave", occurs in the expression used by the Maya to record the first action of the gods in bringing the Fourth Creation into being. Creation texts record *hal k'ohba*, "they wove the image". Depending on the text, the image that was woven in the sky could be a Cosmic Hearth or a Great Turtle, both of which were in the constellation of Orion. Once the constellations were woven and painted onto the sky, the gods spun

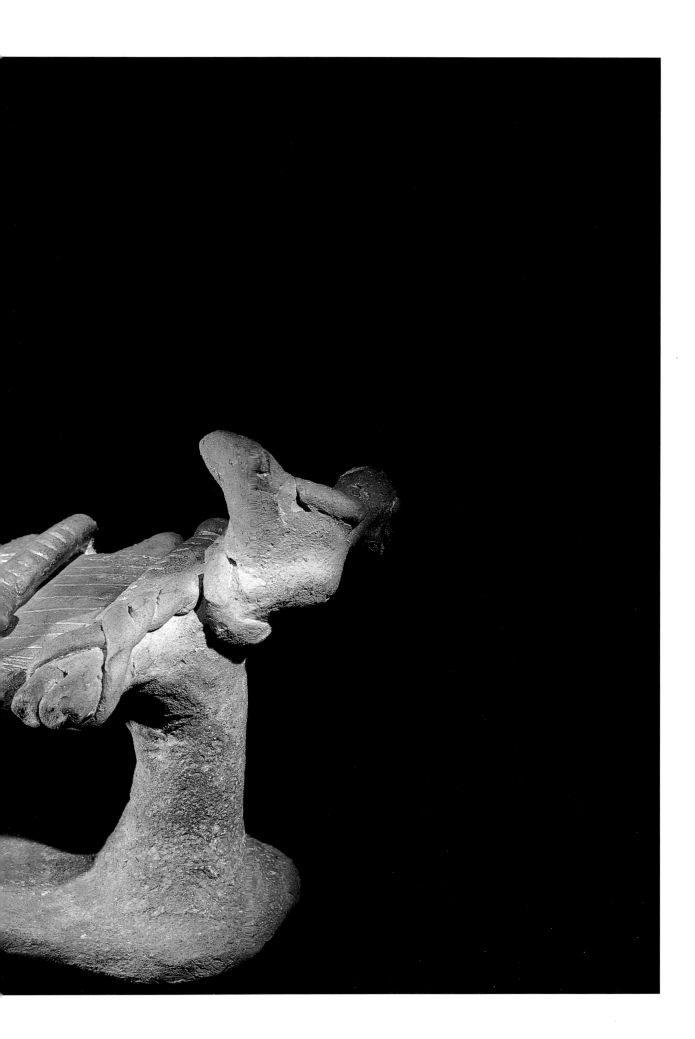

the constellations in the motion of a spindle-whorl, a *pet* or *petet* in Mayan languages. This spinning motion produced time and the motion of the heavens by which time is measured. In Yucatec, "to spin" is *k'uch* and *tol*, while in the Cholan languages, it was *ch'ahna*.

In this figurine (plate 25), the weaver sits with her loom (*halab-te'*) tied to a tree stump with a bird perched on top it. She uses a specially-shaped paddle to tighten the threads she is weaving. The strap of the loom circles her back so that she could lean back or forward to control the tension on the warp threads.

The figurines on the following pages (plates 26 y 27) illustrate two other activities of women, one well known and expected, and

Plate 26 (19 cm) Yale University Art Gallery, Stephen Carlton, B. A. 1903, Fund.

the other more of a surprise. One of these ladies wears an elaborate hair arrangement and headdress, while her *k'ub* drops below her nipples. She leans forward as she works before a round-bottomed vase probably containing a liquid like corn porridge, called *ul* and *sa* by the Yucatecs. In each hand, she holds a round object that may represent tamales (a kind of corn cake), so that the vase could also contain a stew of some kind. Plates with small animals also lay by her knees, although I am not sure

which small animal they were meant to represent.

The second woman holds a folded book on her knee under her right hand. Unlike her counterpart with the pot, she wears a short *k'ub* and a pair of necklaces made of beads. Her clefted, bare upper head probably was once covered with a headdress. Both women have lines emerging from the corners of their mouths, perhaps representing face paint or some other kind of decoration.

Plate 27 (15.6 cm) Museo Nacional de Antropología. INAH/RAICES.

Nikolai Grube, an epigrapher from Germany, recently deciphered a title carried by people in the Maya court. This title (*Ah K'ul-Hun*, "he of the Holy Books") was given to people who kept the books of the ancient courts and lineages in order to record history, tribute payment, genealogies, auguries, and the many other kinds of activities that required written records. Most of the portraits of *Ah K'ul-Hunob* show men, but at Yaxchilan, Lady Eveningstar, the mother of Yaxun-Balam, also carried the title *Na Ah-K'ul-Hun*, "Lady of the Holy Books". This tells us that women, at least those of noble status, could be literate and involved in the keeping of history. This extraordinary figurine depicts another *Na Ah-K'ul-Hun* with her holy book, *k'ul hun*, on her knee.

Two of the women depicted in the next pages (plates 28 and 29) wear their best *k'ub* and jewelry as they carry deep, twisted cloths that very much resemble a ritual scarf worn by men in ritual. Presumably these women

Plate 28 (21.3 cm) Museo Nacional de Antropología. INAH/RAICES.

control that special cloth. One of them (plate 29) once wore a now-missing headdress, while the other (plate 28) has her hair tied with woven bands into an elaborate arrangement on the top of her head. She wears a sheer *k'ub* indicated by blue paint applied to her upper body. Along with her bag, she carries a square object with a double-headed serpent along its top. I do not know what kind of object this represents, but it resembles a special pectoral worn by kings on Altar Q at Copan.

This blue-dressed lady shows yet another important ritual role fulfilled by women in dynastic rituals. Dotted lines cover the edges of her lips and her chin and curve away from the corners of her mouth onto her cheeks. They are identical to dotted volutes that cover the lower face of the famous Lady K'abal-Xok

on Lintel 24 of Yaxchilan. In that scene, the identification of the dotted volutes is clear, because Lady K'abal-Xok draws a thorn-lined rope through her tongue. She offered her blood in a ritual celebrating the birth of an heir to her husband, although the child was not hers.

Lintel 25 of Yaxchilan tells us something more about the bloodletting rites in a way that may explain the presence of women in the accession scenes at Piedras Negras. Lintel 25 shows conjuring rites that took place on the occasion of Itzam-Balam's accession. His principal wife, K'abal-Xok, perforated her tongue, pulled rope through it, and on that occasion conjured up the great War Serpent called Waxaklahun-Ubah-Kan. From its upper mouth, she called out Yat-Balam, the founder

Plate 29 (_ 3 cm) Museo Nacional de Antropología. INAH/RAICES.

Plate 30 (16.5 cm) Museo Regional de Campeche. INAH.

of her husband's dynasty, and from the lower head she materialized the headdress of war. If this Yaxchilan image represents a typical definition of authority that can be applied to other sites, women may have had extraordinary responsibility for and control over the ancestors of their husbands.

Old women also had important roles in Maya life as caretakers for children, midwives, and as sources of wisdom. The prototypical old woman was Chak-Chel, the midwife of Creation, who poured out the flood that destroyed the last Creation and facilitated the birth of the Maize God at the beginning of this one. The following figurines (plates 30-34) depict old women with their sunken breasts and wrinkled faces.

Four of the women (plates 30, 31, 32 and 34) wear twisted bands in their hair, which must have been mostly gray by their age. Smiling enigmatically, one (plate 30) holds a shallow cup in her hands, while another (plate 31) has

Plate 31 (16.8 cm) Museo Nacional de Antropología. INAH/RAICES.

Plate 32 (11.3 cm) The Art Museum, Princeton University. Anonymous loan.

Plate 33 (15.2 cm) American Museum of Natural History N.W.C. Collections Management Fund (44002110).

Plate 34 (9.5 cm) Proyecto Yaxchilán. INAH.

stuck her figures in her mouth for a reason we cannot discern. Another smiling old lady (plate 32) holds onto a rambunctious youngster in her role as caretaker. A fifth woman (plate 33), now missing her headdress, rubs her hands together as an infant riding in a waist band clings to her back. Today, in the highlands of Guatemala, women tie their infants onto their backs using their *rebozos*.

The most interesting of these old ladies (plate 34) comes from Tomb 3 of Yaxchilan,

Structure 24. Archaeological information about this building is yet to be published, but its inscriptions record the deaths of four people. One was the famous Itzam-Balam (Shield-Jaguar), although he was probably buried elsewhere in a more grandiose building. He died on June 19, 742, while his mother, the first of the three women named in this building, died on August 18, 725. The other two women are Lady K'abal-Xok, who died on April 3, 749, and Itzam-Balam's foreign

Plate 35 (12.8 cm) The Art Museum, Princeton University. Anonymous loan.

Plate 36 (21.3 cm) American Museum of Natural History N.W.C. Collections Management Fund (44002110).

Plate 37 (16 cm) Museo Regional de Campeche. INAH.

wife, Lady Eveningstar, who was Yaxun-Balam's mother. She died on March 13, 751. Of the three women, Lady Pakal, Itzam-Balam's mother, was truly an old lady. Her name includes the title *wak-k'atun Na Kolomte* ("six-k'atun Lady Kolomte"), suggesting that she had entered her sixth *k'atun* of life and was over ninety-eight years old when she died. Perhaps this effigy of an old lady went into her tomb to honor her great age.

The lady with the rabbit (plate 35) is one of several figurines that represent this theme. The lady is probably the Moon Goddess, while the rabbit represents one of the images the Maya saw on the moon. Many myths recorded about the Moon Goddess emphasize her licentious behavior, perhaps as a reflection of the moon's quick movement through the constellations and past planets. Although the Moon Goddess's role in the Creation myth seems to

Plate 38 (12.7 cm) Museo del Camino Real de Hekelchak'an. INAH.

Plate 39 (32 cm) Museo Regional de Campeche. INAH.

Plate 40 (16.3 cm) Museo del Camino Real de Hekelchak'an. INAH.

be one of mother and nurturer, this theme of licentiousness seems to be echoed in the image of the Moon Goddess riding the shoulders of a young male. Other figurines (plates 36 and 37) are representations of old or deformed men either hiding in the garments of women or riding their shoulders and tweaking their breasts.

Two figurines in this group (plates 38 and 39) have movable arms and legs. There are a number of these known from Jaina, but we do not know if they were used as dolls or as part of ritual assemblages in which the characters moved during a performance. One of these ladies wears a delicately woven *k'ub* with a triangular cloak on top. This kind of *huipil* also appears on a third figurine (plate 40) of a woman wearing an extraordinarily large hairdo arching over her head. The "Tlaloc" motifs that often appear on this kind of *huipil* are usually taken to record influence from Teotihuacan. Similar motifs appear on the dresses of women at Bonampak' and other southern sites.

Maya men

Like brilliantly befeathered birds, males in ancient Maya society dressed in far more splendor than the women in their world. Male dress could be simple and consist only of loincloth and appropriate jewelry and headgear, but more often, men bedecked themselves from head to foot with elaborate arrays of rich materials and symbols that signalled their status, rank, affiliations, families, personal names, roles in dance drama, and supernatural associations and protections. We will look at the figurines of men to investigate their clothing and the many roles they played in Maya society as they were captured in the figurines.

The simplest dress worn by men was an *ex* or loincloth. Made of finely woven cloth often highly decorated, the *ex* wound around a man's waist and went through his legs to be tied in the back or side with a wide and longer flap covering the front of his loins. When they wore a narrow *ex*, their buttocks remained fully exposed so that male modesty was also very different than today. Men could wear only their *ex*, but more often they also wore necklaces with pectorals often made of jade or carved shells to signal their status and wealth. They also wore earflares made of precious materials carved to represent flowers. Parents changed the shape their babies' heads by flattening their forehead. Since this reshaping could only be done to an infant, the elongated head became a recognizable mark of high status, and adults wore nose pieces to

accentuate the arch of their nose and emphasize the distinctive profile that resulted from their flattened foreheads.

The man depicted in this figurine (plate 1) wore a small chin beard to identify himself as a mature man to be respected because of his age. Maya men have very light facial hair and usually cannot grow beards until their middle and late twenties. His headdress also marks this man as a person of status. Nicknamed the "spangled headdress", it was worn by scribes, educated people, and officials of the court. It consisted of a long woven cloth wound around the head like a turban with shell pieces sewn to the cloth to make the spangles. Feathers often arched out of the top of the headdress.

Men wore many different types of *ex*, including a hipcloth that wound around the entire body. Often brilliantly colored, these *exob* could have designs woven, painted, or dyed into them (plates 2 and 3). For coolness, men often wore nothing on their upper bodies, but always their jewelry included necklaces, earflares, cuffs on wrists and ankles to display wealth and status.

Footgear consisted of sandals made of leather soles tied onto the foot by straps of leather. The sandals could have only straps or a high leather panel around the heel and ankle. Called *xanab*, sandals could also carry symbolic information about the men who wore them.

Plate 1 (27 cm) Museo Nacional de Antropología. INAH/RAICES.

Plate 2 (24.7 cm) National Museum of the American Indian, Smithsonian Institution. 21/5673.

Plate 3 (12.2 cm) Museo del Camino Real de Hekelchak'an. INAH.

Men tied their *exob*, be they simple loincloths or larger hip cloths, in many different ways. The differences may have resulted from custom or from personal references. In the paintings of Bonampak', the color and patterns of the *exob* vary enormously, while on figurines like these they tend to be plain, with the color blue indicated as edging bands or as the entire color of the cloth.

In the headdresses, however, we find many different types and ways of tying them. Brightly colored cloth could be wound around the head in many different patterns (plate 4). The inscriptions call head wrappings *pixom* and headdresses of more solid construction were *hun* or *hunal*. They signalled rank and often included the name of the person who wore them, or carried the images of the gods they embodied. There is enough variation in the *pixom*-type head gear to suppose also that individuals could tie their headwraps in the fashion that they preferred. Most important, many of the headdresses represented in the sculpture of Chich'en Itza do not have counterparts in the imagery of the southern lowlands. However, they do in the figurines and at Bonampak', but only because the figurines and the characters in the famous murals represent far more ranks and functions that those found

Plate 4 (19.4 cm) Museo del Camino Real de Hekelchak'an. INAH.

Plate 5 (19 cm) Museo Regional de Campeche. INAH.

Plate 6 (18.7 cm) National Museum of the American Indian, Smithsonian Institution. 21/5674.

on the public monuments commissioned by kings and lords.

Called *suyem* by the Yukateks, capes were also important ceremonial clothes for Maya men and sometimes for women. Plain capes, like the ones worn by two of these figurines (plates 6 and 7), are rare in Maya imagery. More often the cloth or leather of the cape served as a mounting surface for cut shell or thin jade plaques arranged in rows.

The net pattern of another cape (plate 5) consisted of strung cylinders and beads of jade. In this example, as with the skirt worn by the king depicted on Copan Stela H, the jade net has no backing so that the shoulders or underskirt can be seen through the net. This jade net was worn by men and women portraying First Father (the Maize God) and First Mother (the Moon Goddess). This lord wears a necklace and pectoral over his cape and he has shell sewn to his *ex*.

The lord on plate 7 wears a hip cloth and plain cape, along with a very long scarf wound around his neck and dropping to the ground. This piece of cloth is very rare in Maya imagery, matched only by the long scarf worn by

the short man in the Group of the Cross at Palenque.

Two of these men wear cloth headdresses tied in cylindrical form with panaches of feathers rising from their summits and from the sides. One cylinder has blue cloth woven with the pattern of a turtle's back (plate 5). The Yukatek called women's skirts made with this pattern *ak bon*, "turtle painted". The other headdress (plate 6) has two large rings mounted above a center band made of plaques. This pair of rings occurs on a sacred headdress carried by a feathered serpent on the Temple of the Feathered Serpent at Teotihuacan. The Maya borrowed this symbol for their own headdresses and used it to mark warriors and administrators of the court. The man wearing it on this figurine must have been a court official.

I have often wondered how Maya lords moved when they wore their most elaborate costumes, so burdened were these in symbols and finery. This first of the next group of figurines (plate 8) depicts a lord dressed in his finest. Large earflares made of jade frame his face and his rectangular mouth ornament. A similar ornament made of plaster and

Plate 7 (11.5 cm) American Museum of Natural History N.W.C.
Collections Management Fund (44002110).

Plate 7, rear view (11.5 cm) American Museum of Natural History N.W.C.
Collections Management Fund (44002110).

Plate 8 (16.9 cm) Museo Nacional de Antropología. INAH/RAICES.

painted red was placed over Pakal's face when his people buried him in the Temple of Inscriptions at Palenque. At Dos Pilas, this mouth ornament occurs with the guise of the Maize God in his role as a dancer.

This lord has a removable headdress featuring a zoomorphic head that may belong to the great bird known as Itzam Yeh or Mut Itzamnah. The headband tied to its forehead confirms the identification. The center disk is a flower reading *itz*, the Yukatek word for sacred substances like dew, oozing tree sap, milk, sweat, and dripping candle wax, and for "enchanting" and "making magic". This man is a religious official and perhaps a king.

He wears a heavy multi-stranded collar made of jade beads over his shoulders and a belt supporting a double row of oliva shells that must have sounded as he walked. His belt (*t'et'* or *xok*) supports a backrack that fans

out behind him bearing the head of yet another god. These backracks at most sites carried a symbolic image of the universe. His *ex* peeks out from under his belt and overlays his sandals (*xanab*), this time made in the high-backed style. This man may be dancing, for he holds his bejeweled arms extended out in front of him.

The second lord in the group (plate 9) wears an elaborate and apparently heavy set of clothes. His headdress (*hunal*) has a zoomorphic monster head with a row of jade cylinders and beads just under its jaw. A band with three large flowers surrounds its forehead. Thick panaches of feathers of varying length emerge from the top and sides of his *hunal*. The man wears large ear ornaments and a set of false monster teeth overlays his mouth, held in place by straps tied over his ears. This kind of mouth ornament is very rare.

Plate 9 (20.4 cm) Museo Nacional de Antropología. INAH/RAICES.

He wears an *uh* (collar) of heavy jade beads made into strands of different sized beads. A bib-like flap hangs from it overlaying his belt and *ex* (hipcloth), which has a tasseled fringe. He wears cuffs on his wristlets, knees, and ankles, as well as *xanabob* (sandals). The bag he holds in his left hand is typical gear for many Maya rituals. Most interestingly, feathers emerge from behind the man's arms suggesting that he wore a backrack, but we cannot confirm this because this is a mold-made figurine. The sculptor pressed clay into a mold to get the front and side detail, but he left the back of the figurine plain.

The next figurine (plate 10) is extremely important because of its headdress (*hunal*). The rest of his dress consists of a large jade cape (*suyem*) worn over a thick belt (*xok*) and stiff hipcloth (*ex*). Standing in high-backed sandals, he holds his right hand up in a gesture of greeting. His rectangular nose ornament seems to be held in place by a strap tied around the back of his head, although the strap is now visible only on one side of his face. This kind of nosepiece was very popu-

Plate 10 (24.6 cm) The Art Museum, Princeton University. Gift of J. Lionberger Davis.

lar at Teotihuacan, and later adopted by the Itza who ruled Chich'en Itza during the eighth and ninth centuries.

His enormous headdress has the upper and side fans of feathers, while the main section has a lower cylindrical section made of the turtle-pattern cloth we have seen in other figurines. Blue painted medallions with tassels overlay it under a wide upper band that mounts three more medallions. The band medallions carry blue-painted birds hanging with their heads downward. These are lovely cotingas (*Cotinga amabilis*) known as *yaxun* in Mayan and *xiuh tototl* in Nahualt. Many scholars have identified these birds as Toltec features, but here they appear on the headdress of a man dressed in pure Maya regalia. Moreover, lovely cotingas are a forest canopy bird found throughout the Maya lowlands, but not in the Mexican highlands. This lord is Maya and not an invader from central Mexico.

However, both the cotingas and this odd nose ornament appear frequently in the imagery of the Itza warriors and lords of Chich'en Itza and Uxmal. The *k'atun* histories of the

Plate 11 (24.7 cm) Museo Nacional de Antropología. INAH/RAICES.

Books of the Chilam Balam record that a branch of the Itza confederacy called the *Tutul Xiw* left the region of Tabasco near Jonuta and Palenque to migrate northward. During their migrations, they stopped in the region near Jaina at sites like Xkalumk'in, but eventually moved further north to rule at Uxmal during the late eighth and early ninth centuries. Perhaps this figurine represents one of these lords in regalia that would come to identify members of the Itza confederacy. At Uxmal and Chich'en Itza, they declared themselves to be descendants of the original people who invented civilized life. The Aztec called these original people the Tolteca or "People of Cattail Reeds". The Maya called them *Ah Puh*, also "People of Reeds".

This man (plate 11) wears a large head-dress with flowers and feathers mounted on a cloth base. His hair has been pulled through the headdress to hang down his back with small jewels, perhaps made of jade, attached to the long locks. A large jade collar covers his shoulders and chest, while a necklace hangs to his waist. He has a wide *ex*, a thick belt, and he appears to be wearing an animal pelt over his buttocks and legs. Ballplayers often wore this sort of leather skirt. His sandals have high backs and the sort of strap pattern used by the Maya for many hundreds of years.

The next group of figurines (plates 12-16) shows men of various ranks and roles wearing some kind of application on their cheeks and jaws. I do not know what the application was nor how it was attached to the face. The surface is always shown to be rough, the color is yellow, and it had considerable

Plate 12 (19.5 cm) The Art Museum, Princeton University. Gift of J. Lionberger Davis.

thickness so it could not have been paint. Sometimes the Maya applied it in a non-symmetrical pattern. Unfortunately this face decoration does not appear to my knowledge in any images on stone monuments, so I do not know whether to interpret it as a signal of rank, status, or ritual context.

However, I can identify the roles of at least three of these figurines by using other signals. Two of the people (plates 12 and 13) were court officials and probably scribes, *Ah Tz'ib*, or book keepers, *Ah K'ul-Hun*. The "spangled" headdress that one of them wears (plate 12) identifies him as a scribe or sage, *itz'at*. He also wears hanging disk ear ornaments (*tup*) and a necklace (*uh*) made of jade beads. His *ex* was woven in a two color pattern.

The second man (plate 13) holds a fan in his right hand as he crosses his arms. His collar (*uh*) is mostly gone, but the impressions from the beads still remain to show where it was. He has wrapped a *pixom* (head cloth) around his head and bound it in place with a twisted cloth. He has thrust a round cluster of small sticks under the left side of the twisted cloth. This cluster of sticks appear regularly in the headdresses of court officials depicted on pots, where the text calls them *Ah K'ul-Hun*, "He of the Holy Books". I think this cluster of objects consists of carefully chosen reeds that were cut to the same length and then bound by paper or cloth strips to be carried by scribes and book keepers. When they needed a new pen, they simply drew out one of the reeds and cut it to the shape and fineness they

Plate 13 (17.8 cm) Museo Nacional de Antropología. INAH/RAICES.

Plate 14 (22 cm) Museo Regional de Campeche. INAH.

needed for the job. When it was exhausted, they simply threw it away and prepared another. When not actually working, they stuck the bundle of blank reeds into their headband, much in the way a modern bookkeeper puts his pen or pencil behind his ear.

The remaining figurines with the facial patch (plates 14-16) wear simple *exob* along with a headdress characterized by a twisted hairdo. Two of them (plates 15 and 16) have a band with a series of banana-like objects attached to it. A large spondylus shell hangs over the chest of one of them. Spondylus shells like this, mark administrators of the rank *sahal* at Yaxchilan and Bonampak'. *Sahalob* were appointed by kings and could be the rulers of towns and villages within a larger kingdom or serve as administrators at the court of their overlord. These three have designs on their foreheads with two of the symbols representing portals to the Otherworld.

The spondylus shell pectorals on five of the next group of seven figurines identify them as middle-level court officials.

Plate 15 (20.6 cm) Museo del Camino Real de Hekelchak'an. INAH.

Plate 16 (24 cm) Munson-Williams-Proctor Institute, Museum of Art, Utica, New York.

73

Plate 17 (17.2 cm) The Art Museum, Princeton University. Museum purchase.

One of these figurines (plate 17) wears a turban headdress with an *itz* band marking him as a "sorcerer" and another (plate 18) wears an animal headdress. The others arranged their long hair into twisted or stiffened locks on top of their heads. They all wear wraparound hipcloths, and most have a headband or some other kind of binding thongs in their hair.

All of them have imagery applied to their faces in raised lines that may represent face painting. I suggest the lines represent paint because tattooing or scarification would be permanent. When we have more than one portrait of a person with this kind of facial decoration, such as with the women of Yaxchilan, the decoration comes and goes with the ritual. It appears to have been applied in temporary media.

The heads of three of these figurines (plates 17, 21 and 22) appear to have been made in the same mold. All have a skeletal

Plate 18 (20.1 cm) Museo del Camino Real de Hekelchak'an. INAH.

Plate 19 (19.4 cm) National Museum of the American Indian, Smithsonian Institution. 23/8368.

Plate 20 (16.7 cm) Museo Regional de Campeche. INAH.

Plate 21 (17.8 cm) Museo Nacional de Antropología. INAH/RAICES.

Plate 22 (17.8 cm) Museo del Camino Real de Hekelchak'an. INAH.

lower jaw painted around their own lower jaw and the same pattern of hair and beard. Presumably the skeletal features refer to a Death God or one of the skeletal *nawals* know from Maya imagery.

Two other men (plates 18 and 20) have very similar facial features and small chin beards, but their facial designs are far more elaborate around their eyes. Lines with beads circle the eyes. A third man (plate 19) has the face of GI, one of the three patrons gods of Palenque, painted over his face as if it were a mask. In fact, the facial painting of all six of these figurines transform their human features into divinity faces. It seems that facial paint could serve the same function as face masks for the purpose of procession and dance.

The last, standing man (plate 23) wears a very unusual scalloped *ex* and his *hunal* (headdress) consists of a spangled cloth ar-

Plate 23 (13.8 cm) Museo Nacional de Antropología. INAH/RAICES.

ranged to hold his stiffened hair up on top his head. His bearded face has different symbols painted or attached to each side. On his left cheek, he has a *pop* (mat) sign and on the other, radiating double lines emerging from a central circle. I am not sure what this sign represents. These and many other figurines demonstrate how the Maya used painting and other body decoration to change their aspects for different rituals contents and roles.

Our next figurine (plate 24) is one of the most elegant ones we have. It represents a lord, probably a king, elegantly seated on a now-missing bench with one leg bent under him while

Plate 24 (34.3 cm) American Museum of Natural History N.W.C. Collections Management Fund (44002110).

the other overhangs it. Wearing a simple *ex* and sleeveless jacket, he looks to his right and downward toward something that once sat in his line of view. He wears a flower suspended over his forehead from a headband that is visible only in the paint. His long hair locks hang down his back (not shown), hiding the strap supporting his bar pectoral. The sculptor gave him a pointed head so that he could wear a separately made hat with a high peak. Perhaps this graceful figurine was once part of an assemblage that laid out all the members of this man's court much like the palace scenes recorded on pottery and on Piedras Negras Lintel 3.

Plate 25 (11.3 cm) Museo Nacional de Antropología. INAH/RAICES.

The headdresses and hair arrangements represent the most interesting detail of the next two figurines (plates 25 and 26). They depict men wearing turban-like headdresses (*hunal*) with three *yaxun* (lovely cotinga) birds attached to the upper band. One of these headdresses is removable. It has a vertical fan of feathers attached behind the birds, and the rear view of this headdress shows that it was a hollow cylinder tied at the rear of the head. Headdresses much like these appear with great frequency in the imagery of Chich'en Itza, where they have been associated with "Toltec" imagery. Here the cotinga bird occurs in clearly Maya contexts that preceded Chich'en in time.

Three of the next four figurines (plates 27, 28 and 30) sit in the cross-legged position,

Plate 26 (15.3 cm) Museo Nacional de Antropología. INAH/RAICES.

Plate 26 sin tocado (15.3 cm) Museo Nacional de Antropología. INAH/RAICES.

Plate 27 (11.5 cm) Yale University Art Gallery, Collection of Thomas T. Solley.

displaying a Maya sign of respect: one hand touches the other forearm or shoulder. All wear high-waisted *exob*, some of which are blue or have blue borders. One of them (plate 27) has a multi-stranded necklace with counterweights hanging down his back to balance the heavy weight of the jade (not shown). Most have wrist cuffs and ear ornaments, but the figurine from Palenque (plate 28) has a slim-waist characteristic of the style of that site. It could be that the material used for their *exob* was thinner and lighter in weight than those used in other kingdoms.

One man (plate 27) wears his hair pulled back behind his ears and tied in the back of his head. Another (plate 29), who wore a now-missing headdress, has a full mustache and chin beard. The strangest hairdo occurs on the Palenque figurine (plate 28). The front locks seem strangely disarrayed and the long hair on the rest of the head is bound and stiffened so that it stands up and bends forward.

Plate 28 (16.5 cm) Museo de Sitio de Palenque, Chiapas. INAH.

Plate 29 (16.1 cm) Museo Nacional de Antropología. INAH/RAICES.

Plate 30 (22 1 cm) Museo Nacional de Antropología. INAH/RAICES.

The last man (plate 30) wears cut-shell earflares (*tup*) and a single-strand necklace of medium-sized beads. His headgear consists of a *pixom* (headcloth) held in place by a band tied in the back. The band has disks and a flower sewn to it. He looks like he has just tasted something sour, but the line of beads along his chin may explain his expression. These beaded lines represent blood so that he may have just perforated his tongue. The strange expression on his face may be one of pain.

Plate 31 (29.2 cm) Museo Nacional de Antropología. INAH/RAICES.

This figurine (plate 31) from Simojovel, Chiapas, a town south of Palenque, is larger than many of the others. The seated man wears a plain *ex*, but he has five strands of rope tied around his left wrist and more twisted strands worn around his neck. He also wears a *pixom* tied onto his head by a plain band. Normally, rope would signal a captive, but at Copan, Yax-Pasah, the last king, wore ropes in a special dance of dedication for one of his buildings. This man is not being restrained, and he seems quite calm and self-contained. I do not think he is a captive, but he may be engaged in a ritual requiring self-sacrifice or a rope dance. The most unusual feature of this figurine is a cross-shaped opening to give access to its hollow interior for some unknown purpose. Perhaps offerings were placed inside.

88

Plate 32 (15.1 cms) (throne 10.5 cms) The Art Museum, Princeton University. Gift of Gillett G. Griffin.

This figurine (plate 32) once had a removable headdress that sat on top its head, so that the apparent bald-headedness was not part of the original design. He wears flower earflares (*tupob*) with cylinders representing the stamen extending outward. His plain *ex* lies under a very unusual cape, constructed with three flaps in a style that may once have derived from Teotihuacan dress.

He sits on an extraordinary throne that incorporates powerful symbolism from the Maya story of Creation. The image on the back of the throne represents the Maize God surrounded by maize leaves. The Maize God supervised the Fourth Creation in which the first act was to set up a Cosmic Hearth in which fire was kindled and the world centered. He directed his divine associates to lay the stones of this hearth in the constellation of Orion where he had been reborn from a cracked turtle shell that corresponds to the belt stars. The hearth is the triangle of stars dropping from the belt and the Orion Nebula is the fire.

The names of the three stones of the hearth were the jaguar-throne stone, the snake-throne stone, and the crocodile- or shark- throne stone. A top view of this throne shows it to have the form of a jaguar. It represents the first stone of the hearth: the jaguar-throne stone, sitting here under the god who ordered its erection. The Maya lord who sat on this throne placed himself on the jaguar-throne stone of Creation.

The gorgeous figurine in the following pages (plate 33 and detail) was found in Group B of Palenque, located below the escarpment dropping down to the plain in front of the city. Benches with four slab legs exactly like this one can still be seen in several of the subterranean corridors of the Palace. This figurine clearly shows that they served as seats for

Plate 33, side view (22.4 cm) Museo de Sitio de Palenque, Chiapas. INAH.

Plate 33 (22.4 cm) Museo de Sitio de Palenque, Chiapas. INAH.

lords occupied in the business of the court and in ritual performances. This elegant lord wears a simple *ex*, jeweled cuffs, and a jade necklace as he sits cross-legged in the center of the bench. His left hand rests on his knee as he reaches up with this right hand toward the beak of the extraordinary bird mask that he wears. The strange knobs on the head of the bird and the wattle on his beak identify it as an ocellated turkey, called a *kutz* by the Maya.

Bench-thrones also had backs, although most scenes painted on pottery show the backs to have been made of pillows or panels mounted in walls. Two of the figurines that follow (plates 34 and 35) have benches with glyphic texts molded into the edges of their seat, backs, and on their slab legs. Unfortunately the texts are not legible. The third seat (plate 36) is composed of a plain cylindrical base with a back. All three people seated on these benches wear their *exob* in the form of hipcloths, and have earflares, necklaces, and cuffs on their wrists. Two of them (plates 35 and 36) sit in the cross-legged posture, while the third (plate 34) had folded his legs under him.

The befeathered headdresses are the most important symbolic cues to the roles each man fulfilled. Two lords (plates 34 and 35) wear huge jawless snake heads with their faces emerging from the gullet of the creature. One

Plate 34 (12.3 cm) National Museum of the American Indian, Smithsonian Institution. 23/9947.

serpent is plain, while the other has a mosaic skin, perhaps made of cut-shell. This Mosaic War Serpent is a familiar symbol in Maya art, especially on the war stelae of Piedras Negras, a kingdom on the Usumacinta River. There and throughout Maya art, the Mosaic Monster was a symbol of war, shared by the Teotihuacanos of western Mesoamerica. The two lords depicted in these figurines are wearing the War Serpent as demanded by their roles as war leaders.

The headdress of the last man (plate 36) appears with particular frequency at Chich'en Itza, although it also occurs at other sites, including Piedras Negras and Tikal. The cut feathers of the headdress lie in overlapping parallel rows with a flower sitting above the man's left eye. At Chich'en Itza, this headdress appears on the divinities depicted in the Upper Temple of the Jaguars. Since this flower can be read as *itz*, the headdress may signal that this man is an Itza. This is the name of a group of people who lived around Lake Peten-Itza in the central Peten of present-day Guatemala from the Early Classic period onward. Itza is also the name of the people who settled and ruled Chich'en Itza.

Plate 35 (11.5 cm) Museo de Jonuta. Instituto de Cultura del Estado de Tabasco.

Plate 36 15.5 cm) Museo Nacional de Antropología. INAH/RAICES.

93

SOLDIERS AND WARFARE

War played a big role in Maya life during the Classic period. As with all war, it had economic and political implications because the winners became richer and the losers poorer. Losers paid tribute to the winners and lost control of territory, while winners extended their political control and won access to the resources of the losers.

Maya kingdoms organized themselves into large alliances headed by the great powers of Mutul, as Tikal was called, and Kan, as Kalak'mul was called. Allegiance to and position within these alliances could change as individual lords sought advantage over their neighbors or protection against enemies. The adage "an enemy of my enemy is my friend" and its opposite played themselves out a hundred times during the Classic period. Vengeance and the repaying of old debts were commodities in the politics of the time.

Yet the Maya did not frame their explanation of war in terms of economics or politics. To them, war was a sacred affair played out on a larger battlefield. They transformed into their *wayob* or animal-spirit companions and went to war in supernatural form. They carried their protector gods with them into war so that defeat signaled abandonment by those gods. In fact, the gods could be captured and thrown down to wrest away the supernatural protection of the defeated.

Although men of all ranks went to war, the elites had special interest vested in the outcome. Texts recording the capture and sacrifice of kings demonstrate that Maya rulers did not stay at home and send the youths in their kingdoms to war. They went to war themselves until the end of their lives. We do not know much about the Classic-period order of battle, but secondary lords of the rank *sahal* and *ahaw* served as officers. Many of these lords were the equivalent of professional soldiers, and people of all ranks gained great prestige if they took captives during battle.

Soldiers wore a simple *ex* designed not to entangle their legs. The belts holding up their *exob* often had elaborately woven patterns, and they wore a sleeveless jacket that was open in the front. Many of these jackets displayed elaborate weaving patterns, but the jackets seem more valuable for their symbolic value than as armor. The patterns may have signaled rank or other information within a battle order, but we have no information concerning how it might have worked. Other soldiers went into battle bare-chested and often with body paint that may have called upon their protectors or signaled rank and duty. They also used padded-cotton armor to protect their torsos.

Two of these figurines (plates 1 and 2) show soldiers carrying rectangular, flexible

Plate 1 (22.2 cm) The Art Museum, Princeton University. Anonymous loan.

Plate 2 (18 cm) William P. Palmer III collection, Hudson Museum, University of Maine.

Plate 3 (12.2 cm) Museo Nacional de Antropología. INAH/RAICES.

shields that they used to deflect thrown spears and thrusts by opponents. When marching, they rolled up these shields and carried them on their backs. Soldiers carried long-shafted and short-shafted spears with lance heads made from obsidian or flint. They also used spearthrowers, flint knives, slings, axes, and clubs. Often, elaborate headdresses displaying the *way* or animal-spirit companions completed the headgear of a soldier, although the animal forms may well have signaled additional information about affiliation and rank.

These warriors are wearing jewelry to battle, which would have been ripped off if they had been unfortunate enough to be captured. The standing soldier (plate 1) has vo-

lutes painted or smeared on his forehead under the stiffened locks of his hair. The shape of his head suggests he once wore a headdress. Another soldier (plate 2) kneels in a defensive position with his flexible shield in front of his body and an arm cocked as if he once held a spear ready for throwing. The shell on his chest identifies him as a *sahal*, so that he was likely an officer in the army he served.

The warrior with the scalloped hat (plate 3) wears his battle jacket, but his necklace has two large spheres that may signal yet another rank. His face shows the beaded signs of blood so that he is a penitent as well as a warrior.

Soldiers also wore more complex clothing that included armor and signals of rank,

Plate 4 (18.2 cm) Museo Nacional de Antropología. INAH/RAICES.

although today we cannot interpret the full array of symbols they used. As the next figurine (plate 4) shows, warriors could use helmets that covered the entire head, leaving only an opening for the eyes and nose. The intricately woven material that hangs all around this warrior's body may be armor, and he holds a rectangular shield over the left side of his body. Other figurines with full-body protection are known from Lubaantun and unprovenienced collections. Moreover, ballplayers from Oaxaca also wear helmets to protect the head and face.

The two standing figurines (plates 5 and 6) also wear elaborate clothing includ-ing shoulder capes and heavy hipcloths. The first of them (plate 5) also wears a large pectoral, a necklace, earflares, and a wide belt. He has wrapped his hair in a *pixom* and tied his stiffened locks so that they arch over his head. Since victors controlled their captives by grabbing these tied locks, wearing this hairstyle was an act of bravado and challenge to enemies who might try and take this man captive.

The second soldier (plate 6) wears a huge cloth that stands out at an angle from his body as he spreads his arms. The strange cape is held in place by bands tied around his

Plate 5 (28.5) National Museum of the American Indian, Smithsonian Institution. 22/6348.

Plate 6 (15.4 cm) American Museum of Natural History N.W.C. Collections Management Fund (44002110).

buttocks and thighs. His surviving arm is wrapped from wrist to upper arm in protective binding that also appears on ballplayers at Chich'en Itza. The headdress that once covered his bare head is now missing, and his appearance is made more fearsome by the mask he wears. Made from the face skin of a captured enemy, the mask hangs from his ears and covers the lower half of his face. The shrunken head of another vanquished enemy hangs from his neck with its hair fanning out around the face. Maya warfare was ferocious with the consequences of victory and defeat clearly displayed for everyone to see.

When Maya lords went to war, they transformed into their *way* or "spirit companions". To materialize their *way*, they wore full body costumes to strike fear into the hearts of their enemies and the supernaturals who opposed them. The first of these figurines (plate 7) depicts a lord wearing the mask of his Death God *way* as he brandishes an ax in his left hand. His right hand grabs the scalp locks of a helpless captive in order to wrench his head to the side ready for the blow that

will decapitate him. The doomed captive has his upper arms immobilized by a rope tied behind his back. He is diminutive in size to emphasize the horrifying power of his executioner, who carries a giant rectangular shield on his back. Decapitation was a preferred method for dispatching captives.

Another warrior (plate 8) also wears a complex headdress and backrack with many feathers extending around him like arches. He has a necklace and befeathered *ex* and belt, as he holds his hand outstretched at his side. The double tier of feathers in his headdress characterize battle head gear at Usumacinta sites like Bonampak' and Yaxchilan, but the main cylinder shape is usually called a pillbox or drummajor headdress. It appears as the main warrior headdress for Itza warriors at Chich'en Itza. The central element mounted on the cylinder is a four petaled flower. It may read *k'in*, "sun", or it could be an *itz* flower marking this man as an Itza.

A third warlord (plate 9) stands fully arrayed in the most fearsome of all Maya war gear. He is a master of Tlaloc-Venus warfare, a

Plate 7 (17.5 cm) Museo Regional de Campeche. INAH.

101

Plate 8 (14.2 cm) Museo Regional de Campeche. INAH.

Plate 9 (20.5 cm) Museo Regional de Campeche. INAH.

complex of symbols and religious belief shared with the great city of Teotihuacan. The mask he wears is the god called Tlaloc by the Aztecs. In Teotihuacan, the same image is sometimes called the Rain God, but for both the Maya and the Teotihuacanos, this god was involved in war, and for the Maya it was associated with founders and with ancestry. Specifically, their "Tlaloc god" signaled conquest warfare, timed by the stations of Venus and Jupiter.

This lord wears another symbol sometimes called the "Mexican Year Sign" or the "Bar and Trapeze" sign in each feather panache that springs from his body. This symbol appears at Chich'en Itza in a bundle that tied together cycles of five Venus years with eight tropical years. This 5 x 584 / 8 x 365 cycle functioned as the fundamental Venus-Sun-

Ecliptic cycle for all Mesoamericans. He also wears a spherical headdress with a war serpent called Waxaklahun-Ubah-Kan on its summit. Large feather panaches flare out from the sides and top of his headdress. Additional ones on his backrack extend out from behind his arms. The headdress also includes a shell diadem that arches over the mask. The Maya God Chak, who characteristically wears this diadem, is also associated with axes and decapitation sacrifice. The body costume includes a large pectoral, wide belt, *ex*, and sandals. He carries a spearthrower in his right hand and a bag in his left.

The following figurines (plates 10-13) depict warriors wearing the Mosaic War Serpent that is so prevalent in the war imagery of Piedras Negras and other Classic-period

Plate 10 (21 cm) Munson-Williams-Proctor Institute, Museum of Art, Utica, New York.

Plate 10, sin tocado (21 cm) Munson-Williams-Proctor Institute,

Museum of Art, Utica, New York.

Plate 11 (͞5.5 cm) Museo Regional de Campeche. INAH.

kingdoms. The first of these warriors (plate 10) wears a cape with a long bib overlaying his belt and *ex* as he sits on a rectangular bench. The bib has a head of a perforator god mounted among four spheres. He holds a bag in his right hand and wears elaborate *xanabob*, "sandals", complete with flowers. Large earflares frame his face, which is completely hidden when he wears the mask of his *way* or spirit companion, and its attached head-

dress. The gaping mouth of the huge Mosaic War serpent rises above the mask to dominate the headdress. The small objects arching around the War Serpent have small wings. They are the diving *yaxun* birds (lovely cotinga) so important at Chich'en Itza.

The same kind of *yaxunob* and Mosaic War Serpent mount the headdress of a second figurine (plate 11), depicting a masked warrior holding an ax ready in his right hand. The

Plate 12 (13.9 cm) Museo del Camino Real de Hekelchak'an. INAH.

mask shrouding his face has zoomorphic features and a beard, and he seems to be preparing for battle rather than engaging in it. The leather cape that covers his shoulders and chest frequently occurs in war figurines, although the cut of the cape can change.

A third figurine (Plate 12) with an animal mask shows another kind of cape, with flaps covering his chest and dropping down his shoulders in a style that appears on Tikal Stela 13 and at Teotihuacan. He wields an ax in his left hand, while his right holds a small bag. The

sculptor of this figurine liked detail: he showed the pattern woven into the man's cape and the texture of the feathers in his headdress.

A seated warrior (plate 13) wears the same kind of flapped cape as his sits with his skirt spread over his round stool. He has a backrack made of bound feathers stuck into his belt as he gazes out from under the same Mosaic War Serpent.

Soldiers and kings also wore a headdress that resembles a drummajor's hat. Called a *kohaw* in the inscriptions of Piedras Negras,

Plate 13 (20.7 cm) Museo Nacional de Antropología. INAH/RAICES.

Plate 14 (22.8 cm) Museo Nacional de Antropología. INAH/RAICES.

the headdress consisted of a tall, hollow cylinder that could be made of many different materials. At Chich'en Itza, this war helmet was shorter and three large, black-tipped feathers were worn in a down ball attached to the wearer's hair. Warriors tied them around their heads with small knots at the back. At Palenque, the king received this headdress along with the flint-shield of war during his accession ritual. To become king was to tie on this helmet. These two soldiers (plates 14 and 15) are not kings, because soldiers as well as kings wore this helmet. Interestingly, both men wear huge pectorals, probably made of complex knots and both carry bags in their right hands. They wear sandals, *exob*, and waist-length capes. They may be officers of the army or of the court.

The Maya carried their lords and their patron gods to battle in giant palanquins. At Tikal or Mutul, as the ancients called it, these palanquins consisted of a platform carried by men using a pair of long poles thrust through the platform. Stairs mounted the platform to

Plate 15 (27 cm) National Museum of the American Indian, Smithsonian Institution. 23/3781.

Plate 16 (19.2 cm) Museo Nacional de Antropología. INAH/RAICES.

Plate 17 (27.5 cm) National Museum of the American Indian, Smithsonian Institution. 23/2216.

a seat where the king sat. A gigantic statue of a patron god or *way* (*nawal*) hovered over him to protect him from enemies. According to the texts on the lintels that portray these litters, the warriors of Mutul captured the jaguar palanquin appearing on Tikal's Lintel 3 (Temple 1) from Kalak'mul, just as their ancestors had captured the Mosaic War Snake on Lintel 2 of the same temple from Waxaktun. Later armies captured the snake palanquin from El Peru (Lintel 3 of Temple 4), and the giant jaguar-man from Naranjo (Lintel 2). The victors and their descendants paraded these captured palanquins on many occasions throughout the subsequent history of Mutul.

These two figurines (plates 16 and 17) depict the same kind of palanquins. The two holes that once accommodated carrying poles flank small stairways that lead up a seated lord. The imagery of both palanquins reflects war, but in different ways. In one of them (plate 16), the ruler sits under a towering jaguar being wearing an ornate headdress, a cape, and a necklace with three spondylus shells. This jaguar *way* went to war with its owner. Interestingly, its headdress resembles a war symbol on the east building of the Nunnery Quadrangle at Uxmal.

Plate 18 (22.5 cm) Museo del Camino Real de Hekelchak'an. INAH.

The other figurine (plate 17) shows the ruler sitting inside a frame shaped like a house. The frame has six snake heads attached to it. *Wak-kan* or "Six-Snakes" was the Maya name for the tree that sat at the center of the world and that they saw in the Milky Way. Here the artist realized the name literally as "six snakes", so that this king sits in the middle of the *Wak-Kan* as he rides his palanquin. The roof carries the head of an ancestor wearing the Mosaic War Serpent, and a bird, perhaps a war owl, sits on top. This ancestor is likely to be the founder of the king's dynasty, because of the association of founders with the *Wak-Kan* and this kind of war imagery. Two more snakes emerge from behind the founder opening their mouths to emit bifurcated tongues. All of the snakes have feather fans to identify them as war serpents.

Palanquins could also serve to transport bundles of founding ancestors like the one depicted on Stela 40 of Piedras Negras. In that scene, a living ruler sprinkles an offering into a hole that leads to a chamber under the floor. The bust of an ancestral figure wearing a Mosaic War Serpent and a flapped cape rests on a bench. A twisted rope representing an umbilical cord emerges from his nose to rise up through the hole into the space of his descendant above.

Plate 19 (19.7 cm) Museo de Jonuta. Instituto de Cultura del Estado de Tabasco.

Plate 20 (14.8 cm) Museo de Jonuta. Instituto de Cultura del Estado de Tabasco.

Plate 21 (16.3 cm) Museo Regional de Campeche. INAH.

The four figurines that we will now talk about (plates 18-21) are representation of similar bundles of ancestors. The first of these bundles (plate 18) consists of a masked person who is wearing the headgear arrangement known as the Mosaic War Serpent headdress and the same flapped cape. The bundle rests on a palanquin enabling it to be carried in public processions. Two additional figurines (plates 19 and 20) from Jonuta show similar ancestral figures, who are wearing the same clothes, but without the mask. They are sitting on benches with the same hieroglyphic inscription, although unfortunately neither text is readable. A fourth figurine (plate 21) does not wear the cape and shows more of the body, even though no legs or arms were modeled. This too represents an ancestor bundle, probably containing the remains of the founding ancestor of the lineage that commissioned it. The last three figurines we have analyzed show their respective bundles resting on a bench similar to the one shown on Stela 40.

Captives taken in war could look forward to humiliation, torture, and slavery or death. The five figurines that follow (plates 22-26) are portraits of some of the unfortunate

114

Plate 22 (16.3 cm) Museo Nacional de Antropología. INAH/RAICES.

losers of war. Two of the figurines in this group (plates 22 and 23) depict captives who display the pot bellies and sagging muscles of middle-aged men who were probably of high social rank. With his hands bound behind his back, the man with the beard(plate 23) looks toward his right with a look of resignation on his face. The other middle-aged captive (plate 22) has his genitals exposed and a grimace on his face. A third figurine (plate 24) is also totally naked and sits on the floor, with his hands tied behind him and his eyes severely swollen. These last two captives have both been beaten and have been stripped of their clothing as part of their public humiliation.

Another captive (plate 25) writhes in the agony of torture, although his arms and the post he was bound to did not survive.

One of the most extraordinary figures (plate 26) shows a naked captive hanging from a stand of modern construction. Scenes in the murals of Mulchic, a site near Uxmal in Yucatan, show dead captives hanging from trees and others are executed by stoning. The fate of captives was not pleasant, but Maya men went into war knowing what could happen to them.

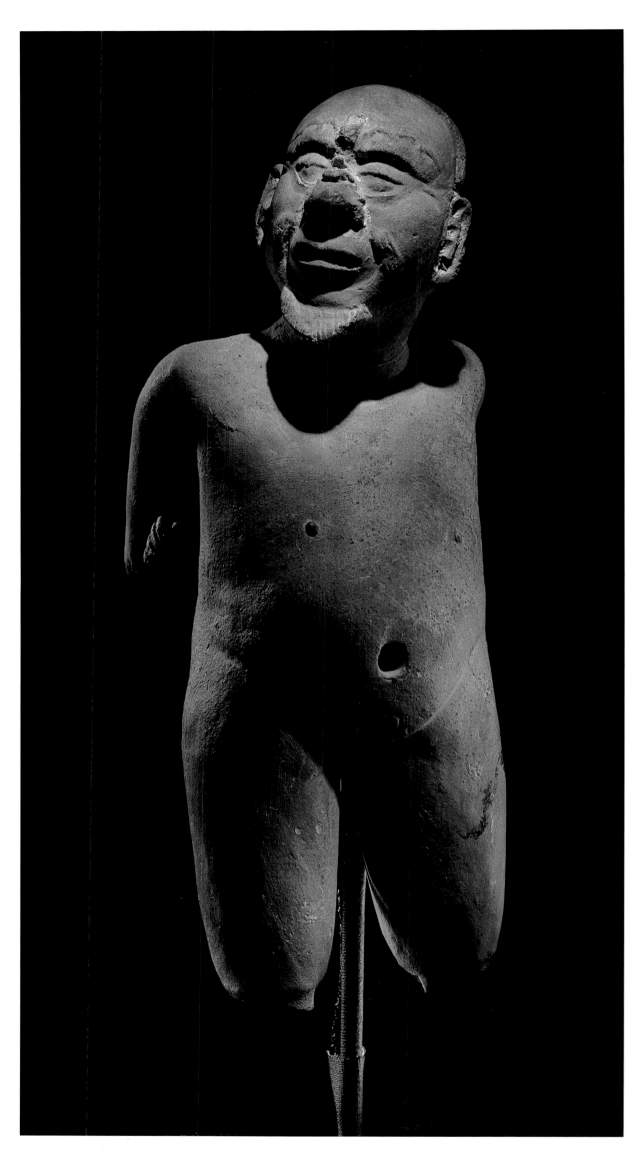

Plate 23 (19.5 cm) The Art Museum, Princeton University. Anonymous loan.

Plate 24 (10.4 cm) The Art Museum, Princeton University. Anonymous loan.

The *Rabinal Achi*, a post-conquest drama that is still being performed by a lineage in the Guatemalan highland town of Rabinal, tells the story of a captured spy who knows he faces a terrible death at the hands of his captors. Offered a way out of his terrible fate if he agrees to betray his people, he chooses death with honor. The same ideas about honor and destiny very probably played an important part in ancient Maya concepts of war and its consequences. And not all captives died. They could become slaves or choose to accept the authority of their captors. In fact, one of several ship-wrecked Spaniards captured by the Maya in the years before the conquest survived to become a great Maya warlord who made war on his countrymen until the day he died. Thus, we can presume that the captives of ancient times could also survive and become subjects of their captors.

Plate 25 (21.5 cm) The Art Museum, Princeton University. Anonymous loan.

Plate 26 (16.2 cm) The Art Museum, Princeton University. Museum purchase, bequest of Helen Hamilton Maier and Henry William Maier, by exchange.

THE BALLGAME

The Maya, like all other Mesoamerican peoples, played a game with a rubber ball. Called *pitz*, the game lay at the heart of the religious and political lives of the Maya. It provided one of the central metaphors of the Maya Creation story. Conceptually, the ballcourt was the crack on top of the Mountain that held the maize kernels used to create humanity at the beginning of this, the Fourth Creation. Moreover, the ballcourt provided the arena in which the Lords of Xibalba killed the Maize Gods and buried them. There, the miraculously conceived twin sons of the Maize Gods come to resurrect them and bring them back to life. And when the Maize Gods were reborn, they stayed in the ballcourt where human beings come to honor them.

The ballgame also provided an environment for the negotiation of alliances, for lords to journey into the Otherworld to consult oracle gods and ancestors, and for sacrificing captured kings and high lords At Chich'en Itza, the ballcourt contains narrative murals that record the establishment of the Itza confederation both in historical time and at the moment of Creation, the conquest wars that gave them the right to rule, the sanctification of warfare, the myth of the Maize Gods and their sons, and the legitimate transfer of political power from one ruler to the next. The ballcourt and the game were central to Maya politics and religion.

Ballplayers wore special equipment to protect them during play. A heavy leather skirt hung from their belts to shield the buttocks and legs from the impact of the ball and burns from skidding on the pavement of the playing ally. The seated ballplayer shown in the following page (plate 2) wears one of these made from the pelt of an animal whose head was included in the finished skirt. He holds a small stone in his right hand that may have been used to start the ball in play. Hand stones like the one this figurine holds are known from archaeological contexts.

To protect the ribs and pelvic bones from contusions, players wore a yoke, called a *bate* in the inscriptions, around their waists. Many stone ones are known, but the actual playing yoke was probably made of wood. In fact, in Tikal Burial 195, archaeologists found a wooden yoke very much like the ones worn by these figurines (plates 1 and 3). Another object called a *palma* could be attached to the front of the belt (see plate 1), but we do not know how the Maya used these strange objects in their game. The Maya carved these thinly cut stones into images of animals, humans, or gods.

Ballplayers also wrapped padding around their forearms and wore a knee pad

Plate 1 (18.5 cm) Yale University Art Gallery, Stephen Carlton Clark, B. A. 1903 Fund.

Plate 2 (14.5 cm) Munson-Williams-Proctor Institute,
Museum of Art, Utica, New York.

Plate 2, back view (14.5 cm) Munson-Williams-Proctor Institute,
Museum of Art, Utica, New York.

Plate 3 (14.2 cm) Museo del Camino Real de Hekelchak'an. CNCA/INAH.

Plate 4 (14.4 cm) Museo del Camino Real de Hekelchak'an. CNCA/INAH.

123

Plate 5 (14.3 cm) Museo Nacional de Antropología. INAH/RAICES.

(see figure 6), although usually only on one knee. They also wore many different kinds of headdresses, but especially favored large animal heads that may have represented their *way*. One of these players wears a giant owl head as his headdress (plate 4).

One extraordinary figurine (plate 5) shows a ballplayer frozen in the typical posture of play. He wears his leather skirt, a *bate* (yoke), knee pad, and forearm wrapping. He has thrown himself onto his padded knee and lifted his arms away from the yoke, that he can catch the flying ball and send it back toward an opponent. Apparently, neither the hands nor feet could touch the ball, and the pattern of play called for players always to go down on the same knee. The ball could bounce on the floor of the alley, hit markers set into the floor or mounted on the alley walls, or it could ricochet off the angled benches that lined the alley.

The other player (plate 6) wears a deer head as part of his headdress, along with his

Plate 6 (24.8 cm) William P. Palmer III collection, Hudson Museum, University of Maine.

yoke and his knee pad. However, play has not begun, because this player still holds the ball in his hand. The rubber ball is about the size of a soccer ball, but in many of the stone reliefs it was much larger. Images at Yaxchilan suggest that the game began with vision rites conducted by important women, although we do not know how the game itself started. Teams had multiple players on each side (as few as two and as many as six), but we do not know how they scored in the game, by what rules they played, or what happened if they won. If they lost in the games of major political and religious import, they died by decapitation or by being thrown down stairs (at least according to the images and myths about the ballgame that have survived from the Classic period). The modern myth that the Maya sacrificed the winner has no support in the ancient sources. However, the Maya very probably also played their ballgame for sport and as entertainment for kids and adults.

RITUALS AND DRAMA

In ancient times, the Maya filled their lives with rituals and public pageants of many kinds and sizes, just as they do today in the traditional communities that dot the landscape of Central America. Many figurines show people engaged in these rituals although, because individual figurines do not appear in scenes, we have to rely on narrative images on pots and on Classic-period stone monuments to identify the particular rituals. The Maya used a complex calendar system to track history, to identify the symmetries inherent in the seasons and astronomical phenomena, and follow the actions of the gods in the past, present, and future. As complex as the Catholic saints' calendar or as the Hindu ritual calendar, the Maya system provided frequent and repeated occasions for ritual at the family, lineage, community, and kingdom levels. Maya life was a rich tapestry of rituals, celebrations, healing rites, festivals, and divinations.

At the center of most Maya rituals was the dance, *ak'ot*, as it was written in the glyphs. Kings and nobles as well as villagers and farmers danced holding objects and wearing costumes appropriate to the occasion. In most contexts, the Maya depicted their dance by raising the heel of dancers' feet and showing hands in formal position. However, the dance could also lead to states of ecstasy and trance. One of these figurines (plate 1) shows the heel-up position, while a second (plate 2) depicts a dancer throwing out his arm and arching his back as he moves through his dance, apparently in a state of trance.

The dance and other rituals led to the transformation of the dancer or shaman into his animal-spirit companion, called a *way* by the Maya.

Plate 1 (12.5 cm) American Museum of Natural History N.W.C. Collections Management Fund (44002110).

Plate 2 (17.9 cm) Museo Nacional de Antropología. INAH/RAICES.

The figurine on the next page (plate 3) shows a dwarf dressed in a blue-feathered bodysuit. People who wear this suit are often pot-bellied and appear to have had a special religious function. Here, the dwarf holds a fan under his raised forearm, as his *way*, who is perhaps a coatimundi, emerges from his back. Notice that the *way* also has a human body and that the gestures on the two sides of the figurine mirror each other. This is a depiction of two aspects of one person: his human persona and his *way*.

One of the most frequent transformations involved birds (perhaps because trance states often make people feel like they are flying). Bird dancers often wear feathered-body suits and masks that completely hide their heads (plates 4-7). The transformation into birds was "real" to them as they entered trance states, but the full-body suits also aided in the

Plate 3, three views (10.9 cm) The Art Museum, Princeton University. Anonymous loan.

effectiveness of large public pageants. Vultures and owls, both powerful birds of omen, were particularly important *wayob*. Dwarves as well as full-sized adults could transform into these bird *wayob*.

Transformational figurines sometimes show the mask that a celebrant wore during the ritual. One such figurine (plate 8) shows a person wearing a duck mask that covers his entire head. However, his very human eyes gaze out from the large eye-holes of the mask. He also wears an ornately woven skirt and an ankle-length cape that opens to reveal his round stomach. Cut cloth with flapped openings like the ones in this character's cape often show up in scenes of sacrifice and bloodletting. He carries a deer antler in one hand and an unknown object (perhaps a small turtle shell) in the other. He may be playing a drum as he undergoes transformation.

Plate 4 (15 cm) Museo del Camino Real de Hekelchak'an. INAH.

Plate 5 (16.9 cm) Museo de Jonuta. Instituto de Cultura del Estado de Tabasco.

Plate 6 (17.4 cm) Museo de Jonuta. Instituto de Cultura del Estadao de Tabasco.

Plate 7 (15.5 cm) National Museum of the American Indian,
Smithsonian Institution. 24/3405.

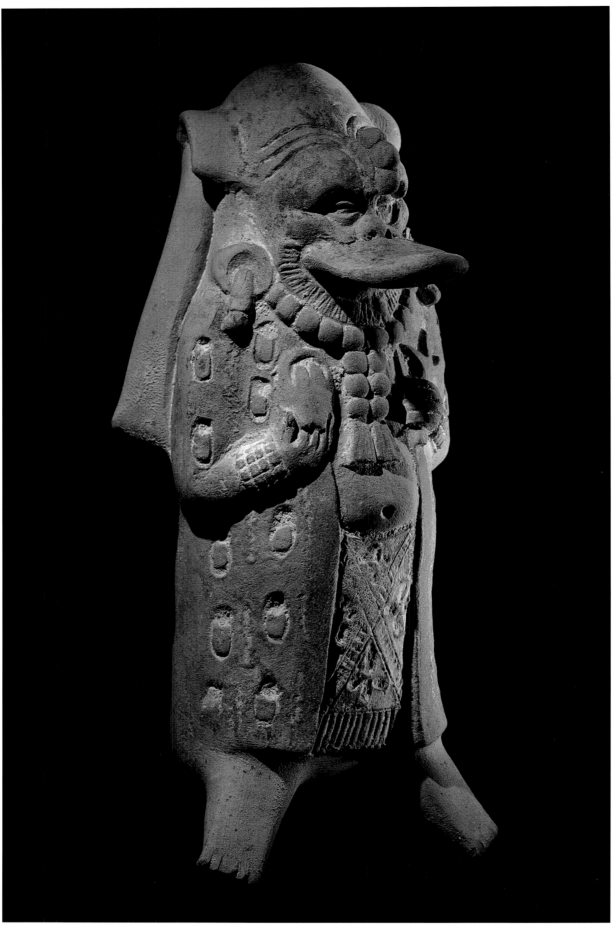

Plate 8 (16.1 cm) Museo Nacional de Antropología. INAH/RAICES.

The faces of the next two figurines (plates 9 and 10) are elongated into the wrinkle-skinned heads of howler monkeys. Both these monkey-men wear necklaces of twisted cloth. A least two female figurines carry almost identical object in their hands so that they may be shown bringing these cloth objects to men who will transform into monkeys as part of their ritual performance. Both of these monkey men carry rattles, so that they may also be musicians.

Ch'ulel, the living force that imbues the universe, resides in human blood, making it one of the most sacred gifts the Maya could give to their gods and their ancestors. Blood was taken from captives and animals, but individuals also gave their own blood in voluntary auto-sacrifice. They two most favored

Plate 9 (13.4 cm) Museo Regional de Campeche. INAH.

Plate 10 (15.4 cm) Museo del Camino Real de Hekelchak'an. INAH.

Plate 11 (19.7 cm) American Museum of Natural History N.W.C. Collections Management Fund (44002110).

Plate 12 (17.1 cm) The Art Museum, Princeton University. Museum purchase, gift of Leonard H. Bernheim, Jr.

areas of the body for particularly important offerings were the tongues of both men and women and the penis for the male. Moreover, from descriptions at the time of the conquest and from a figurine group found at Santa Rita, we know that bloodletting rituals involved many men at once and that warriors could participate in these rituals as well.

The next four figurines depict the ritual of penis perforation and its aftermath. One of them (plate 11) presents an elegantly dressed man wearing a rope around his neck. His penis lies outstretched on paper as he cuts into the spade-shaped glans. His face shows no pain as he proceeds with his offering. Another figurine (plate 12) shows a seated man with his erect penis extending from his body. His hands are now empty, but perhaps he once held the perforator in his outstretched hand as a separate sculptural piece.

Plate 13 (8.3 cm) Museo de Balancán. Instituto de Cultura del Estado de Tabasco.

Plate 14 (8 cm) Museo de Jonuta. Instituto de Cultura del Estado de Tabasco.

Not all men who took blood from their genitals suffered the ritual with the same stoicism. A small figurine from Balancan (plate 13) shows a man squatting with one knee up as he touches his perforated penis. He holds his other hand against the side of his head as he screams out his pain. Another figurine (plate 14) shows the same scream, but the man's body is entirely shrouded by his cloak. I cannot be sure why he screams, but he likely has also given blood.

From these four figurines we learn that this important ritual could be suffered with stoic disregard for the pain or with screaming distress. Perhaps men gained and lost prestige according to how much pain they displayed during the ordeal.

People undergoing bloodletting rituals also wore special costuming. The man shown overleaf (plate 15) has removed his stone ear ornaments and replaced them with long paper strips. Scenes painted on pottery show pa-

Plate 15 (24.8 cm) Yale University Art Gallery, Collection of J. B. Rapp

Plate 16 (22 cm) The Art Museum, Princeton University. Anonymous loan.

per strips just like these splattered with red spots, so that this man is a penitent. Blood from ears, face, arms, and legs also had value as offerings.

Hand-woven cloth cannot be cut without unraveling so that Maya weavers always shaped their cloth as they wove it on their looms. The one exception was clothing worn in bloodletting rituals. Three of these figurines (plates 16-18) show this kind of cut material.

One figurine (plate 16) shows a man wearing a cut-cloth garment with holes cut in rows, with the cut cloth used as a flap. His headdress has blue-painted leaves spraying out around his head. The cloth from the cut holes flaps open in a pattern frequently show in bloodletting contexts.

Another figurine (plate 17) wears a long kilt and a cape made of cut strips. These kinds of capes were also worn by warriors and kings in war-related rituals. This man's face is covered with blood emerging from both his mouth and his ears. He has perforated his tongue to give blood from the place where speech is made.

Still another figurine (plate 18) shows a man carrying flapped cloth over his arm for use in a ritual.

One of the most important activities in ancient Maya society had to do with rituals was divination. The four surviving codices, for example, provided divinations for the days of the 260-day calendar in relationship to many different activities.

Plate 17 (18 cm) Yale University Art Gallery, Gift of the Olsen Foundation.

Plate 18 (24.5 cm) Museo Nacional de Antropología. INAH.

Plate 19 (14.4 cm) William P. Palmer III collection, Hudson Museum, University of Maine.

The first figurine in this group (plate 19) shows a man wearing an owl headdress as he carries a book-shaped object under his arm. Owls were birds of omen and associated with war. The object under his arm may well be a book used by diviners.

The second diviner (plate 20) wears a bird headdress also, but his bird has a flower trapped in his beak. The object in the man's hands is a mirror. During the Classic period, such divining mirrors were made of hematite and other metallic stones or obsidian glued onto wooden or stone backings. By the time

of Chich'en Itza, they could also be made of gold and of turquoise mosaics. Mirrors created portals by which ancestors, Vision Serpents, and other supernatural beings entered the world. They also let diviners and rulers see deeper realities than those of the everyday world.

A third figurine (plate 21) is larger than the others and may have functioned as an incensario stand. It depicts a person who has facial hair, a thickened waist line and the wrinkled face of an older man. His necklace, with three spondylus shells, identifies him as

Plate 20 (14.3 cm) National Museum of the American Indian, Smithsonian Institution. 22/5598.

Plate 21 (28.9 cm) Museo de Sitio de Palenque. Chiapas. INAH.

a court functionary. The zoomorphic monster head under his feet rises up to enfold his body in the form of a portal into the Otherworld. The Maya opened these portals by giving offerings and by burning incense in order to feed the gods and their ancestors.

Another figurine (plate 22) shows a person standing in front of a cylinder that looks very much like those used in censer stands. The gender of this person is not clear, although the skirt suggests a woman. The clothing includes six narrow cloth bands that have been tied around the chest and ribs. This kind of binding appears in bloodletting scenes at Bonampak' and in the accession ritual depicted in the Group of the Cross at Palenque.

Maya ritual included feasting and drinking that went along with the dancing and other activities. The first figurine in this group (plate 23) shows a man who seems a little inebriated.

Plate 22 (⌐5.5 cm) Museo Regional de Campeche. INAH.

Plate 23 (36.5 cm) National Museum of the American Indian, Smithsonian Institution. 23/2579.

He holds a double-chamber pot in his hand as he rubs his chin. The woven belt around his waist and his loincloth have fallen very low on his paunchy body.

Another seated man in this group (plate 24) holds a cylindrical vessel under one arm. It may be a container of some sort, but the Maya also made ceramic drums of this size and shape. Perhaps he plays a drum for dancers. An additional figurine (plate 25) shows a man holding his wooden trumpet. The stick

visible along the front of the trumpet served to suspend the fragile bell of these huge instruments while they were played. Since no finger holes are shown, the musician probably controlled tone and note with his lips and air pressure.

One of the most enigmatic actors in the imagery of northern Yucatan is a person who is shown wearing a full-body suit made of either feathers or padded-cotton armor. Many figurines depict people dressed in this strange

146

Plate 24 (9.8 cm) Museo del Camino Real de Hekelchak'an. INAH.

Plate 25 (17.7 cm) Museo Nacional de Antropología. INAH/RAICES.

Plate 26 (18.5 cm) Museo de Jonuta. Instituto de Cultura del Estado de Tabasco.

suit (plates 26-28), which also appears in the monumental art of Yucatan. We do not know if the suit signals a particular office or a repeating role in a unknown ritual, but the feather-suited figures are often pot-bellied.

Often people wore this kind of suit next to their skin and put their *exob* and other accouterments over it. People who wear it can be young and handsome or they can have deformed faces and bodies. The cloak could also be worn as a cape.

Warriors also wore feather suits in warfare rituals and perhaps in battle itself. A warrior (plate 26) wears a feather backrack and an animal head mask. Another (plate 27) car-

ries a round shield and may once have had a spear in his other hand. Notice that both men wore their *exob* over their feather suits.

Dwarves also wore the feather suit during their activities. We have already seen one transforming into his *way* (page 129). That dwarf and the pudgy one in this group (plate 28) both carry fans, but this one does not have a visible *way*. The fat-bellied character with puffy cheeks that appears on page 53 also wears this kind of feather suit, as he adopts an unusual posture: he rides the shoulders of a woman, who reaches up to steady her rider's body. The puffy-cheeked fellow takes advantage of the moment to caress her breast.

Plate 27 (20.6 cm) Yale University Art Gallery, Stephen Carlton Clark, B. A. 1903 Fund.

Plate 28 (14.2 cm) National Museum of the American Indian,
Smithsonian Institution. 23/3780.

Dwarfs and duendes

Dwarfs played important roles in the events leading up to the Fourth Creation as helpers of the Maize Gods. Pottery scenes showing dancing Maize Gods depict dwarfs dancing with them. They also had dwarf helpers when they woke up the Paddler Gods, who paddled them to the place of Creation in Orion, as did God L, the old deity who destroyed the Third Creation by flood.

In the inscriptions, the glyph for "dwarf" reads *ch'at* or *k'at*, depending on whether the inscription was Cholan or Yucatecan. Another word for dwarf, *ak*, is the same as the word for turtle and peccary (both important to the story of Creation). Dwarfs also carry the title *Ah Mas*, while modern Yucatec Maya call dwarfs and hunchbacks *p'us*. Modern stories speak of a race of little people called the *p'usob* who lived in a prior Creation with the Itza, another ancient race of people who were wise and who built the great buildings at Chich'en Itza and Coba. When the ancient paradise of a previous time ended in flood, the Itza were banished to the earth below the ruins of the ancient cities where they still dwell today. The hunchback dwarfs (the *p'usob*) died by drowning when their stone boats sank. Their boats still exist as the old grinding stones that litter the ancient ruins.*

These beliefs have their origin in Precolumbian times. For example, the Dresden Codex shows the destruction of the last Creation by floods brought on by the old Moon goddess, Chak-Chel, and God L, a god of war and merchants. Other Maya groups, such as the Tzotzil and Tzeltal believe that a race of dwarfs lives inside the earth. Thus, Maya peoples associate dwarfs with the interior of the earth, caves, and with beings who lived in a past age. To the ancient Maya, they were *duendes*, who helped the Maize God in the Fourth Creation. The ancient kings apparently saw dwarfs as living embodiments of those mythic supernatural helpers. Dwarfs aided kings on earth just as the original dwarfs helped the Maize God at Creation. They served food, were musicians, carried the sacred objects of the king, and worked for the court as diviners and sages. Perhaps more importantly, as denizens of the inner earth and helpers of the Maize God, they were particularly good companions to send with a dead relative beginning his journey into the Otherworld.

---

* Robert Redfield and Alfonso Villa Rojas (1962:12) recorded the roles these stories played in the lives of the people of Chan Kom. The P'usob are well known to Maya people throughout Yukatan.

Plate 1 (12.5 cm) The Art Museum, Princeton University. Gift of J. Lionberger Davis.

Plate 2 (10.8 cm) Museo Regional de Campeche. INAH.

The very similar clothes of three of the dwarfs shown here (plates 2-4) suggest they all held the same office or function. They all wear an *ex*, a round pectoral, large round ear ornaments, and an animal headdress. The animal heads, a bird and two deers, are all worn with the animals turned sideways on the head.

Almost all the dwarfs in this section (plates 1-13) wear the same clothing, but their headdresses and pectorals correspond to those of court officials. The shell pectoral especially marked people of high rank who served the king. The turban headdresses also appear on courtiers who had many different responsibili-

ties. Dwarfs often served food and brought special objects that their lords required during rituals. The headdress that looks like a folded napkin (plate 5) was called a *pixom*, (head wrap). This kind of *pixom* was often worn by sages and scribes.

These dwarfs also served in a court. One of them wears heavy eyeplates that usually mark gods (plate 1), as well as long, thick mustaches, something that is unusual in Maya imagery. He carries the square shield of a warrior and the high-peaked hat associated with hunters, so that he may have served a group specializing in those activities. Another dwarf

Plate 3 (9 cm) William P. Palmer III collection, Hudson Museum, University of Maine.

Plate 4 (11.5 cm) American Museum of Natural History N.W.C.

Collections Management Fund (44002110).

Plate 5 (10.6 cm) The Art Museum, Princeton University. Anonymous loan.

Plate 6 (10.8 cm) American Museum of Natural History N.W.C.

Collections Management Fund (44002110).

Plate 7 (9.4 cm) Museo Nacional de Antropología. INAH/RAICES.

Plate 8 (11.1 cm) Museo Nacional de Antropología. INAH/RAICES.

Plate 9 (21.1 cm) The Art Museum, Princeton University. Anonymous loan.

Plate 10 (19.1 cm) Museo Nacional de Antropología. INAH/RAICES.

156

Plate 11 (12.⁻ cm) Museo del Camino Real de Hekelchak'an. INAH.

Plate 12 (11.⁻ cm) American Museum of Natural History N.W.C.

Collections Management Fund (44002110).

Plate 13 (20.9 cm) Museo Nacional de Antropología. INAH/RAICES.

(plate 9) wears the shell pectoral that marks court functionaries and a wrapped turban with an animal head emerging from its summit. Turban headdresses like this appear frequently in pottery palace scenes and at Chich'en Itza.

The final figurine in the dwarf group (plate 13) depicts a complex palanquin, complete with holes for the carrying rods. The palanquin body has the stepped contour of a ballcourt with bird heads mounted on the upper corners of the court. The building atop the ballcourt doubles as a giant headdress for the ballplayer figure sitting in the cleft. He wears full ballplayer regalia, including a yoke, knee pad, and wrapped forearm. Two dwarfs sit at his feet in the same position as the dwarf helpers of the Maize Gods. The Maize Gods died and were reborn in the ballcourt, so that these dwarfs may represent their helpers (the original *p'usob* who survived into modern myth).

In ancient times, people with deformities from birth defects and disease could also play crucial roles in ritual and the court. The Maya revered such people, because they made figurines of them to place in the graves of their loved ones and to use in rituals. The figurines in our next group depict people with distorted features and bodies.

Plate 14 (124 cm) Museo Nacional de Antropología. INAH/RAICES.

The first of them (plate 14) shows a man with a bulbous nose and coarse features quite unlike the elegant beauty admired in men belonging to the nobility. He crosses his arms with one of his hands resting on a shoulder in the gesture used by the Maya to show respect and acknowledge subordination. The fan he is shown holding could be carried by court officials and religious practitioners.

The face of a second man (plate 15) shows a serious distortion in the eye area. This could very probably be due to a birth defect. A profile view shows that he has virtually no bridge to his nose and he also has puffy cheeks. His narrow shoulders seem to be too small for his very wide hips. Often, these kinds of distortions signal captives who have been submitted to torture or beaten, but in the case of these two figurines, both people are clearly free and of high status.

Another figurine (plate 16) depicts a person dressed in a very elaborate costume who is perhaps engaged in dance.

The last two figurines in this group (plates 17 and 18) are depictions of men with hugely swollen bellies and thin, elongated legs. One of them shows a very prominent backbone, while both have puffy cheeks, a feature that is characteristic of most of these figurines.

Plate 15 (15.4 cm) Museo Nacional de Antropología. INAH/RAICES.

Plate 16 (13 cm) Museo Regional de Campeche. INAH.

Plate 17 (20 cm) Museo Nacional de Antropología. INAH/RAICES.

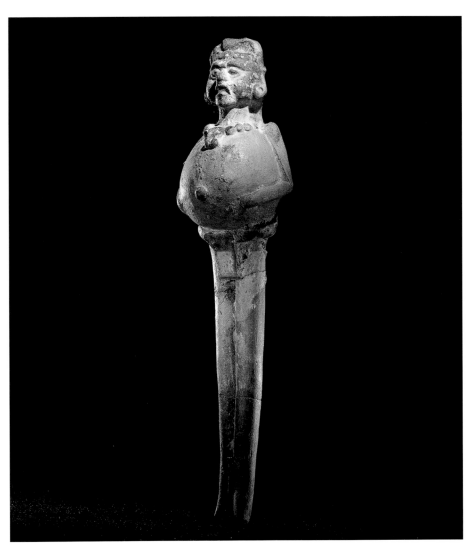

Plate 18 (14 cm) Museo Regional de Campeche. INAH.

GODS AND BEINGS
FROM THE LAST CREATION

Figurines depicted gods and supernatural beings as well as people of the court. In fact, many of the beings who appear in narratives on the pottery of central Peten sites show up in the figurines of Palenque and other sites. Perhaps people put these gods in their relatives' tombs to provide them with supernatural help in their journey after death. These deity figurines may also have been used on altars and in temples as part of rituals of worship, divination, and commemoration.

This jaguar-featured god (plate 1) has been called the Jaguar God of the Underworld and God III of the Palenque Triad. He had several names in the inscriptions, including Hun-Kanal Tzuk Ahaw, (One-Sky Beard-Lord: a Venus god) and K'in-Hix, (Sun-Jaguar: a sun god). In this figurine, the god has jaguar-paw hands, a beard, large eyes, and a screech owl in his headdress. Archaeologists have found this combination of owl and jaguar god at Tikal and Seibal, but this figure is in the style of Palenque. Often, kings wore the guise of this god or carried war shields displaying its face. The brilliant polychrome paint surviving on this figurine gives us some idea of how painted examples originally looked.

An extraordinary figurine (plate 2) depicts an old god with a bird attached to his back. The bird is Itzam-Ye or Mut Itzamnah, as he was named at Xkalumk'in. This old god is therefore Itzamnah presented in a moment when he transforms into his *nawal* or *way*. As the first sorcerer of the Fourth Creation, Itzamnah set up the third stone of the Cosmic Hearth (the shark/crocodile stone throne as-

Plate 2 (14.5 cm) Museo Nacional de Antropología. INAH/RAICES.

sociated with the Primordial Sea). Here Itzamnah's body acts as a container; he carried a liquid inside his body (perhaps to lend magic to important rituals).

The figurine on the next page (plate 3) represents the Old Moon Goddess named Chak-Chel, (Great Rainbow) in the ancient inscriptions. She was the midwife who tended the birth of the Fourth Creation, and along with God L, another old god, she brought on the flood that ended the Third Creation. She wears the twisted hair style that many old women wore. The jaguar ears that sit behind the headdress usually are part of the features of Chak-Chel. The rectangular war shield carried by this old goddess may seem out of place for a midwife, but the Lower Temple of the Jaguars at Chich'en Itza shows other old goddesses dressed as warriors and carrying weapons. She, like God L, her associate, was a warrior deity.

Plate 3 (25.9 cm) The Art Museum, Princeton University. Gift of J. Lionberger Davis.

Our next figurine (plate 4) depicts Pawahtun, the old god who held up the corners of the sky. This deity can be found wearing a turtle carapace, as here, a snail shell, or a conch. He helped Chak-Chel in the birth of humanity after the completion of the Fourth Creation and he served as the patron god of the Itza at Chich'en Itza.

Man-devouring jaguars are rare images in Maya art, but one of the figurines shown overleaf (plate 5) provides a particularly graphic example. It shows a huge jaguar gnawing at the neck of a disemboweled man, whose intestines tumble out of his slashed body toward the ground below. Either the victim is a child or this is a giant jaguar, perhaps like those in Lacandon stories, according to which Celestial Jaguars devoured humanity when the world was destroyed, at the closing of the former Creation. Thus, this figurine may

Plate 4 (8.1 cm) The Art Museum, Princeton University. Anonymous loan.

Plate 5 (12.1 cm) Museo Nacional de Antropología. INAH/RAICES.

Plate 6 (16.3 cm) Museo del Camino Real de Hekelchak'an. INAH.

describe events in the closing m ɔ ments of the Third Creation.

Monkeys were also creatures left over from the Third Creation. The Maya creation myth tells the story of a set of twins who were great artists and artisans. They used to torment their younger twin brothers, the famous Hero Twins. In turning the tables on their older broth-ers, the Hero Twins transformed them into monkeys. They became Hun Batz' and Hun Chuwen, the patron gods of artists, scribes, and artisans.

This monkey (plate 6), however, does not seem to be a scribe. He carries a giant cylinder (perhaps a merchant's pack) in a tumpline. A high peaked hat rests on top of the pack. Most of all, the monkey is quite

Plate 10 (15.2 cm) The Art Museum, Princeton University. Museum purchase.

Plate 11 (12.1 ɔm) Museo Nacional de Antropología. INAH/RAICES.

Plate 12 a,b (5.1 y 6 cm) National Museum of the American Indian, Smithsonian Institution. 24/451 a,b.

clearly a male in a state of excitement. Monkeys, called *maax* in Mayan, often evidence overtly sexual behavior in Maya imagery, as they do in the wild. To the Chamulas of today, people from the outside are *maaxob* left over from the last Creation, because we do not know how to speak or behave properly.

Perhaps this monkey is also left over from the last creation.

The Lacandon also say that their major gods were born from plumeria flowers, called *nikte* by them and by the Yucatec Maya. Classic-period imagery also shows the rebirth of the Maize God from a *nikte*, though in the earlier

period, *nikte* was the word for all flowers. Some figurines (plates 7, 8, 10 and 12b) depict the emergence of young gods from the blossoms of plumeria and waterlilies. Others (plates 9, 11 and 12a) depict the birth of old gods from blossoms. They cross their arms across their stomachs or lay them on the petal in front of them. We do not know who these gods are, but old gods emerging from flowers appear on the west building of the Nunnery Quadrangle at Uxmal and, at Copan, an old god emerges from plant forms on a early building called *Ani*. This imagery, then, occurred on pottery, in figurines, and in architectural decoration.

FIGURINES OF INTEREST

All the people, one man and three women, depicted in the following set of figurines (plates 1-4) wear a high-peaked, wide-brimmed hat. A dwarf (see page 150) and a monkey (see page 167) from earlier pages are also shown wearing this hat. Pottery scenes show the Hero Twins wearing a similar hat when they are hunting, but these people clearly are not hunters. We do not know if the hat is a signal of rank or important in a particular ritual, but the Maya did not normally wear brimmed hats like these.

The first man (plate 1) has an upturned brim and a flower sitting on the peak of his hat. His neck scarf overlays a long, blue-painted cloak.

One of the women (plate 2) reaches up to hold her hat in place, while another woman (plate 3), shown sitting down, has the hat well balanced on her head. The hats of these two women have flattened-peaks instead of the pointed forms of other hats. One last woman (plate 4) holds a cup in her hand and her blouse has fallen off her shoulders to reveal her breasts. Perhaps she is a bit inebriated. A detail (not shown) shows a cloth coming out of the crown of the hat in a style very similar to the hat worn by the Maya of Zinacantan in Chiapas.

The Maya used molds to make their figurines so that sometimes we have more

Plate 1 (26.9 cm) Museo Nacional de Antropología. INAH/RAICES.

Plate 2 (18.6 cm) Museo Nacional de Antropología. INAH/RAICES.

Plate 3 (17 cm) Museo Regional de Campeche. INAH.

Plate 4 (19 cm) Museo Nacional de Antropología. INAH/RAICES.

Plate 5 (18.2 cm) Museo Nacional de Antropología. INAH/RAICES.

than one version of the same figure. The groups that follow (plates 5-11) are cases in point.

The first set of three figurines (plates 5-7) depicts a woman standing in front of a portal made of intertwined rattlesnakes. The feather fans on the snakes' head identify them as War Serpents. Plant stalks overlap the panaches of feathers that extend from the sides of the figurine, while a sideways sky glyph sits amid the upper feathers. *Kan* was the word for both "snake" and "sky", so that the glyph may mark the snake and define it as a heavenly serpent. The first of these three figurines (plate 5) was excavated from Jaina in 1942. The other two (plates 6 and 7) were made with the same mold and are now part of museum collections in the United States. The first example can be documented as authentic because archaeologists excavated it under controlled circumstances. The other two were made from the same mold, but we cannot be sure when.

Plate 6 (18.4 cm) National Museum of the American Indian, Smithsonian Institution. 23/2862.

Plate 7 (17.9 cm) The Art Museum, Princeton University. Anonymous loan.

Plate 8 (20.4 cm) Museo del Camino Real de Hekelchak'an. INAH.

Artists used another mold to make the second pair of figurines (plates 8 and 9). Archaeologists excavated the first one(plate 8) at Jaina, while the second one (plate 9) is nowadays part of the collection of an American museum. Both show a woman dressed in an elaborate woven *k'ub* and *pik*. She holds up her hands in a gesture common to female figurines from both Jaina and Jonuta. In this case, the archaeologically excavated figurine shows more erosion than its duplicate in the United States.

At first glance, the last two figurines (plates 10 and 11) appear to come from the same mold, but they have different sizes (20.1

Plate 9 (20.2 cm) National Museum of the American Indian, Smithsonian Institution. 21/8092

cm versus 16.8 cm) and different details. While they both depict a standing woman, the objects they hold are different. One woman holds a shield with her two hands, while the other lady has one hand at her side and a fan over her chest. Otherwise, the facial features and the details of the jewelry and the clothing are identical. The potters may have used molds to create two master figurines, which they then used to make two additional, nearly identical molds. This technique would account for the differences in detail and size. Such practices suggest the existence of workshops specializing in the manufacture of these figurines.

Plate 10 (20.1 cɪ-1) Museo del Camino Real de Hekelchak'an. INAH.

Plate 11 (16.8 cm) Museo del Camino Real de Hekelchak'an. INAH.

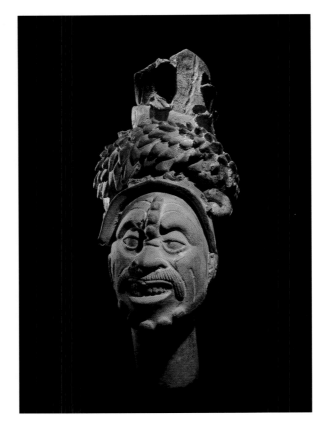

(11.9 cm) Museo Nacional de Antropología. INAH/RAICES.

FURTHER READING

ALVAREZ A., CARLOS, AND LUIS CASASOLA. *Las Figurillas de Jonuta, Tabasco*. Mexico City: Universidad Nacional Autónoma de México, 1985.

CORSON, CHRISTOPHER. *Maya Anthropomorphic Figurines from Jaina Island, Campeche*. Ramona, Calif.: Ballena Press, 1976.

ECKHOLM, SUZANNA. *The Lagartero Ceramic "Pendants"*. In *Fourth Palenque Round Table*, 1980. Vol. 6 (gen. editor, Merle Greene Robertson; vol. editor, Elizabeth Benson, ed.): 211-220. San Francisco, Pre-Columbian Art Research Institute, 1985.

GROTH KIMBALL, IRMGARD. *Mayan Terracottas*. New York: Frederick Praeger, 1960.

RANDS, ROBERT, AND BARBARA RANDS. *Pottery Figurines of the Maya Lowlands. In Handbook of Middle American Indians* 2: 535-560. Austin: University of Texas Press, 1973.

SCHELE, LINDA AND PETER MATHEWS. *The Bodega of Palenque, Chiapas, Mexico*. Washington, D.C.: Dumbarton Oaks, Trustees of Harvard University, 1979.